HEALING YOUR GRIEF

HEALING YOUR GRIEF

Revised Edition

Foreword by
Msgr. Thomas Hartman

♦

RUTHANN WILLIAMS, OP

First published by the Sacred Heart Press, Caldwell, NJ in 1987.

Published in 1995 by Resurrection Press, Ltd.
P.O. Box 248
Williston Park, NY 11596

ISBN 1-878718-29-0

Cover design by John Murello

Printed in the United States of America.

My deepest thanks to

Eileen McGrath, RSM
who planted the seeds

the sisters with whom I lived
Catherine Waters, OP
Trudy Dunham, OP
Marge Jaros, OP
who were patient with me
while it germinated

all the friends
who gave me time and space
for the blossoming

and always and everywhere
my love, my thanks, my praise
to our gracious God.

For my "cloud of witnesses"
all those
whom I have loved
and lost
for now but not forever

Contents

Foreword

Many have written about grief. They announce the stages: shock, suffering, acceptance. They help us to realize that our pain is normal, our guilt is acceptable, our anger and depression are part of the journey. We become disoriented and look at the world for consolation and often find a world too busy or unkind.

Sr. Ruthann presents the landmarks of grief as well as anyone. She's particularly aware of the feelings of the bereaved. She's willing to share personal, painful moments — the death of her father, the suicide of a friend. She helps her readers to get healthy by knowing that they aren't going crazy. Life isn't perfect. Relationships know pain. Grief is a process. It is real. It is individualized. It can't be timed. We're humans. We're not robots. We can feel and hurt and get sad and be sorrowful and be scared. She shares her insights as to what to say and be in the midst of death and what not to say and not to be.

Sr. Ruthann gives the reader permission to cry, to feel abandoned, to get angry. This gift alone would make a reader want to know her, learn from her and read her book. But the real gift of *Healing Your Grief* is Sr. Ruthann's prayer life.

Sr. Ruthann intimates that life can be good, can be on

track. And then . . . suddenly in a moment — or subtly over time, it can be derailed. We can be thrown. The plan is no longer ours. And at that moment, we enter a profound moment of crisis. It is the struggle of humanity. Why am I here? What am I meant to do?

Sr. Ruthann suggests that we're invited to let go, let God. We're confronted with the deepest reality of life — that death is cruel if seen in human terms alone and meaningful if seen through the eyes of faith.

Death invites us to believe, to trust, to pray, to get closer to God. Our life is changed, not ended. We go on. We meet God. We continue to grow. For those of us left behind, death is a mystery. We don't see what the deceased see. We can only believe.

But belief is not solitary. It is not foolish. It's a tapestry of colors that we fill in each day. Sr. Ruthann turns the pages of the Bible in a skillful way to point out how there are precedents for our feelings in the Bible. She invites us to place our trust in God . . . a loving God . . . a merciful God . . . a caring God. The deceased are in the peace and friendship of God. We on earth are also in the peace and friendship of God.

Sr. Ruthann knows the feelings of grief on a personal and psychological level, but she's gone beyond that. She has placed her life in God's hands — in prayer and relationship in this world — and her fate in God's hands for the next world.

MSGR. THOMAS J. HARTMAN
Director of Radio and Television of Telicare
Diocese of Rockville Centre, NY

Introduction

Someone you love has died.

Perhaps the death was expected, perhaps not. It really makes little difference in how you feel now because you are never really prepared for the death of someone you love. But now it has happened. And you are left behind to get on with the business of living even though you feel as if a part of you has died as well.

Someone you love has died.

It is an awesome and an awful experience for you. You are numb or sad or angry or guilty or lonely or relieved. Or all of those things. Or any combination of them. The intensity of your feelings is painful. Or the very lack of any feeling is frightening. Will you ever be — do you ever want to be — "normal" again?

Someone you love has died.

Why did it have to happen? Why now? Why here? Why him? Why her? Why me? And where is God in it all?

Friends reach out to you and you shun them. Your mail sits, unopened. You don't answer the telephone. You don't go out. The sun goes down and you sit, uncaring, in the darkness.

Or you find you can't be alone. You need someone with you constantly. Some distraction to keep you busy. Your television set is on twenty-four hours a day, just for the company it provides. You seize on any opportunity to be with, up, out, and about. There is practically nothing you won't do for companionship. Even the anonymous companions of a movie theater are better than being alone.

Someone you love has died.

The things you do — or don't do — may seem to be irrational, far removed from your ordinary way of being. Are you losing your mind?

No.

Take comfort in knowing that no matter how strange your emotions, reactions, behavior might seem, they are absolutely normal for a person who is grieving. Someone once said that abnormal behavior in abnormal circumstances is normal. This is not an ordinary time for you. Why, then, anticipate that you will carry on in an ordinary way? Unless your behavior becomes truly self- or other-destructive, allow it to happen. Eventually, when you have worked through the wild and storm-tossed terrain of emotions, you will settle back again into more familiar ways of being.

And take comfort in knowing that God is no stranger to what you are experiencing. From King David's crying out over the death of his son Absalom to Jesus' mourning over Lazarus, the people of our religious history have mourned — and have been comforted — and have returned to normalcy.

Oh, there is no doubt that they were changed, as you will — in some way — be changed. To experience the death of someone you love causes a wound, a terrible wound; and every deep wound leaves a scar. But the scar need not be disfiguring if you allow yourself to be healed.

I say "allow" because, of course, we can choose not to be healed. We can refuse medication, bandages, rest. And we can continue to exist with a vicious and poisonous wound. We can most certainly do that. God gave us free will and does not take back his gifts, no matter the cost to ourselves . . . or to him. "Choose life," God says in Deuteronomy 30:19, underscoring that it is always our choice. Choosing to be healed from grief is a definite choosing of life.

And I have deliberately said "to be healed," not "to heal," because I believe that — though we must cooperate by choosing the healing — it is God working through the Son in the power of the Holy Spirit who is the true Healer. It is God who binds up our wounds, cures our paralysis, and infuses us with peace. It is God in the person of Jesus who gives us comfort and rest.

But part of the difficulty we experience in grief and mourning has to do with our time and culture. While this latter half of the twentieth century has brought us many good things, it has also brought us two very unhealthy concepts. The first is that everything may be had or done instantaneously. And the second is that we must at all times and in all circumstances be in control.

The Big Mac Syndrome

The first concept, which I think of as the Big Mac Syndrome, is a product of our instant, freeze-thaw, pre-packed, heat and serve, buy-now-and-pay-later way of living. Madison Avenue and the fast food industry have provided us frequently with needed services. But at what cost to our mentalities! We have come to believe that everything may be taken care of quickly, that we can have all that we want right now. Maybe even yesterday.

But mourning is not like that. It is a process, usually a very slow process, unfolding at the pace the Lord knows is best for us. It cannot be rushed.

The Big Mac Syndrome also affects our mourning at our work place, dictating that if there is a death in the family we may have three days or maybe even five off from work. Then on with life! I can think of few things that are more unrealistic. If my leg is broken, it is expected that I will be in the hospital, in a cast, in a wheelchair, on crutches, and out of work for weeks to allow the leg time to heal. But we make no such allowance for healing broken hearts. Why not? Perhaps it is because of the second concept I mentioned: our need to be in control, what I term the Locked Box Syndrome.

The Locked Box Syndrome

We have learned in our times to control an amazing variety of things: everything from hair color and body odor to the temperature of our houses and the way we pray. We can put our cars on cruise control, run our televisions by remote control, put our shower massage on gentle control, and set lights in our homes on timer control. We have made a minor deity out of control and we worship unashamedly at that shrine. What is more damning than to say that someone is "out of control"?

The Locked Box Syndrome has invaded us at our deepest levels and so we believe that we must, at all costs control our emotions (and that cost is more dear than we imagine—ask any counselor). We fold our emotions up tightly like bits of colored tissue paper and thrust them firmly into a corner of our Locked Box. If we cannot see them, they don't exist, right? Oh, but they do. And unlike bits of paper, they weigh an enormous amount. Gradually, as we continue to stuff them into our Locked Boxes, they become intolerable burdens, bending us over with their weight.

If grief is to be healed, it must be acknowledged. It must be named, felt, and handed over to Jesus. Not even he can deal with a Locked Box. Nor will he cooperate with a Big Mac.

Jesus knows that the crisis you are now experiencing is awesome and difficult and painful. He also knows that mourning is sacred work for we are allowing God to work in us to heal us and make us new. And he also knows that if you give your grief over to him, it can become an opportunity for your growth, a potential time for a powerful experience of the Divine, a passage of healing grace.

Come To Me

Jesus stands, arms outstretched, to love you back into peace and joy. And he has the patience to be with you throughout the journey. He knows your pain. He has felt it himself. He wants to help you through it, to take it upon himself, to make you free again. He whispers to you even now....

> Come to me, all you who labor and are burdened, and I will give you rest. (Mt 11:28)

I will bless the Lord at all times,
his praise shall be ever in my mouth.
Let my soul glory in the Lord,
the lowly will hear me and be glad.
Glorify the Lord with me,
let us together extol his name.
I sought the Lord, and he answered me
and delivered me from all my fears.
Look to him that you may be radiant with joy,
and your faces may not blush with shame.
When the afflicted call out, the Lord hears
and from all distress he saves them.
The angel of the Lord encamps
around those who fear him, and delivers them.
Taste and see how good the Lord is,
happy are they who take refuge in him.
The Lord is close to the brokenhearted;
and those who are crushed in spirit he saves.

PSALM 34

— 1 —

The Mourning Journey

♦

Thus says the Lord of hosts:
Attention! Tell the wailing women to come,
summon the best of them;
Let them come quickly
and intone a dirge for us,
That our eyes may be wet with weeping,
our cheeks run with tears.
The dirge is heard from Zion:
Ruined we are and greatly ashamed;
We must leave the land,
give up our homes!

(Jer 9:16–18)

Grief is not only painful, it is also frightening. And most of us are even more unprepared for mourning than we are for death.

Mourning is not a popular topic of conversation. It's not taught in school, and unless we are curious enough to pursue it in reading, we find ourselves in the midst of it as unfamiliar with its facets as an extraterrestrial being suddenly plunged into Times Square at high noon. The odds are, we have not attempted to learn about it because such a pursuit would be considered "morbid" in this age of recreational drugs and death-defying facelifts.

But we are here now, unprepared and scared and feeling alone. It is bad enough that we are consumed by a pain greater than we could have imagined, that we feel torn apart, that we experience a terrible sense of isolation. But we also discover that our grief has hurled us into an unknown place. We are not extraterrestrials but terrestrials suddenly caught in a time warp, in a twilight zone, in a place we have not been and which we do not recognize.

The Landscape of Grief

The landscape is bleak and barren, a contradiction of a hot, dry winter that we have never known before. And as we find ourselves here in this place which we do not understand, we find also that we are very afraid. Where am I? What has happened? Will I be lost here forever? What is going to happen to me?

What is worse is that we can still see into the "normal" world. People's lives whirl by in their routines of work, play, prayer. There are colors and music out there, and laughter. The familiar is there, all right, all that only a few days ago we were part of. But no longer. Now we are here in this terrifying desolation and we can't rejoin that other world though it is so tantalizingly close—all around us, but so far away. So we stand frightened, hurting, and intolerably alone in the place of our pain.

But though it seems a torment to see that other world and not to be able to be a part of it, there is grace there. It reminds us that the familiar and the comfortable do still exist.

It reassures us that others have loved and suffered and have recovered. And it helps us to remember the beautiful face of God which we have seen and which now probably seems lost to us forever.

That is the promise: the beauty we have known can be ours again, even though in some ways it will be different. As each sunset is unique, so is each moment of beauty that we know and so is our God's way of dealing with us, not anonymously but personally and in just the ways that we need. As tenderly and individually as he created us, so he continues to care for us throughout our lives, the good times and the bad. He is there, hovering above us, swooping below us, always abiding within us to keep us from any permanent harm.

If we can remember that, as we stare out unhappily at the world "passing by," we can be reminded of what is still waiting for us after we have mourned and been healed.

A Simple Map

Perhaps it would help to have at least a very rudimentary map of this new landscape, and that is the purpose of this brief section: to provide a map. It's not the sort of map Triple A makes up, the best route all clearly marked so that we can proceed to our destination smoothly and without encountering delay. Would that it were! But the landscape of mourning is not like that. And the process of traveling it is not easy.

The trip is not necessarily or even probably going to be a regular progression from one point to the next. The signposts are often confusing; and the landmarks, frequently repetitive. There are detours, dead ends, paths that double back to where we have already been, and places where the road is completely washed out and must be reconstructed before we can continue. Sometimes we may even find ourselves — against all logic — in more than one place at a time. But mourning defies logic. It is not a matter of intellect or will, but one of the heart where logic is suspended and feeling allows what is happening, what is to come, what has been. The cool rational world does not intrude here for this is a place of our deepest selves: the place at which we are alone with God.

No Time Limits

There is no time limit, no pressure to hurry and be done with it, no prize to be won if you finish grieving before anyone else. Jesus has all of eternity. He will walk with you for however long your journey takes.

Remember, though you may be back at work just a few days after the funeral, you are not back to being yourself by then. Don't expect it. And don't let others' expectations push you and your emotions into a "locked box." This is your time of healing and you have every right to claim it. More than a right, a very real need.

By the same token, please allow others their time and way to mourn. Do not be surprised that you do not see them in your landscape. The way for each mourner is particularly his or her own and, except for the presence of the Lord, is mostly a solitary way.

Wounds take time to heal and different people heal at different rates. This is just as true for emotional wounds as for physical ones. So be patient with others of your family and friends who are not "in step" with your journey. Some people seem to be more resilient than others. They "snap back" and recover with enviable speed while others are still flattened by the blow. The length of the mourning journey is not a measure of the depth of love, however. It is a personal characteristic, no more a matter of will than the color of your eyes.

Grieving is highly individualistic. Each person brings who he or she is into the process. The result is neither predictable nor uniform. As you have the right to be, so do others. Try to allow that and accept their state of being — and your own — whatever it may be. It is comforting to remember that there are no "shoulds in sadness."

Many psychologists have studied the grieving process. It is from their study that you may identify certain places in your landscape. They are not progressive stages as I have mentioned. Some may recur over and over again on your journey. Some may never appear at all. But it is helpful to name them and discuss them a bit so that when and if they do appear, you are prepared to know them, maybe even befriend them, and certainly accept them as a normal part of what you are feeling.

These landmarks in grieving are shock, disorganization and disorientation, sorrow, guilt, loss and/or loneliness, and anger. We will talk about and pray through these together. And then add one final one which many of the psychologists tend to leave out, but which we as believing Christians may look forward to at the end of our mourning: resurrection.

Though Jesus may seem very far away right now, if and when you can, cling to him. He hears your cry, he feels your pain, and he wants to make you whole again.

You Are My Child

I'd like to share with you, before I close this section, a dream I had which I believe was a message from our gracious God. About three years ago a friend of mine completed suicide. He was young and handsome, and seemed — at least to those who knew him only casually — to be on a joyful and rewarding life path. I knew he was troubled and at Christmas time, via telephone, we made plans to meet in the early spring to talk. One February night he killed himself. And there I was, caught in the unfamiliar landscape of grief with no warning. And loaded with guilt.

My appetite faded. My step lost its bounce. I couldn't sing. And every poem I tried to write ended in tears. I was angry at God (more on that later). I felt that God had abandoned me. Then I had the dream.

I was carrying a cross up a very steep hill, struggling and sweating under its incredible weight. My friend was on the cross, dead. I fell several times under my burden and gradually through my pain I began to wonder if I could ever make the climb alone. Suddenly the weight was lifted. I looked back over my shoulder and saw a man I knew, though I didn't "recognize" him in the ordinary sense, lifting the cross ever so gently from my shoulder and taking it on his own. He smiled. "Let me help you," he said. And I, in my dream confusion, cried out, "No, no. He was *my* friend." "Your friend," he said, "but my child, as you are my child." And immediately, as is the way in dreams, the heavy cross was gone, the hill was gone, and I was in a meadow. Far ahead I could see my friend, no longer dead, but running joyfully toward a great light at the meadow's end. And my "Simon of Cyrene" stood at my side. "He is free and you are free," he said to me. And then he embraced me. At that moment my friend turned, waved to me, and vanished into the light.

It was not an instant cure, no Big Mac Syndrome here. But the next morning I noticed that I was beginning to feel better, and the healing continued through the next few months. The message of the dream was clear to me, as I hope it is to you. Jesus is there, stepping out of the crowd as did Simon of Cyrene to help with the burden of our sorrow. We can refuse his help, of course; but if we will only accept what he is so willing to give, our way out of mourning will be more swift and less sorrowful.

PRAYER

Lord, I am frightened.
I do not know this place where I find myself.
And there seems to be no one here with me
and no sign to show me the way.

Have you abandoned me too?
Or will you come now and walk with me
where I have not been before,
helping me not to stumble too often,
helping me not to become completely lost.

Will you help me with this cross of mourning?
I cannot carry it alone.

Take my hand, Lord.
I need the comfort of your presence.
Take my hand.
I need to feel the pressure of your touch.
Take my hand, Lord.
I cannot stand alone.

Aloud to God I cry:
aloud to God, to hear me;
on the day of my distress I seek the Lord.
By night my hands are stretched out without flagging;
my soul refuses comfort.
When I remember God I moan;
when I ponder, my spirit grows faint.
You keep my eyes watchful;
I am troubled and cannot speak.
I consider the days of old;
the years long past, I remember.
In the night I meditate in my heart;
I ponder, and my spirit broods:
"Will the Lord reject forever
and nevermore be favorable?
Will his kindness utterly cease,
his promise fail for all generations?
Has God forgotten pity?
Does he in his anger withhold his compassion?"
And I say, "This is my sorrow,
that the right hand of the Most High is changed."

PSALM 77

— 2 —

Shock

The earth is utterly laid waste, utterly stripped,
for the Lord has decreed this thing.
The earth mourns and fades,
the world languishes and fades;
both heaven and earth languish...
The wine mourns, the vine languishes,
all the merry-hearted groan.
Stilled are the cheerful timbrels,
ended the shouts of the jubilant,
stilled is the cheerful harp.

(Is 24:3–4, 7–8)

Shock is a stillness and a wasteland, a place of barrenness, a place of timelessness. It is a great nothingness in which all feeling, all sensation, all sensitivity are suspended. Nothing can hurt us because nothing can really reach us. We are barricaded, beyond feeling, beyond pain. In shock, we do not suffer, do not mourn. We merely — and barely — exist. Life in shock is non-life because we are insulated from living emotion.

But shock is also a great protection. It keeps us from hurting and from hurting ourselves further because, in many ways, it immobilizes us, holds us in the tension between past and present so that we are prevented from moving in ways that will worsen the wound.

When a person is severely injured physically, the body reacts by going into shock. In essence what happens is that the brain simply refuses to accept the pain signals that the nerves are sending. Therefore, there is no felt pain. The blessing that this is never ceases to amaze me.

When I was a very small child, a car ran over me, literally, almost severing my foot from my leg. I remember quite clearly lying in the street, unable to stand up. I remember wondering what was wrong. I remember my mother crying, the ride in the ambulance, being wheeled into the emergency room. The one thing I do not remember is pain. Shock had mercifully closed my brain to those signals because the pain of the injury was greater than I was able to bear.

Emotional Pain

This is just as true for emotional pain. Given a hurt too immense for us to stand, such as the death of a loved one, we go into emotional shock. Feeling ceases. We are surprised, perhaps, that immediately following the death of someone we love, we feel nothing. No pain. No hurt. None of the suffering we might have expected. We do not cry or scream or even whimper. Maybe we only stare or find ourselves trying to console the doctor. Maybe we even laugh! Which is not as hard-hearted as it seems.

Think of the last time you were under a great deal of tension. The pressure mounted and mounted until you felt you might explode. Then something happened to bring the tension to an end. In the great relief that followed, the easing of all those tense muscles and joints, you very probably laughed.

Though the parallel might not be immediately apparent, standing a death watch is similar. There is ever-growing tension, and we react physically to that. When the tension is broken, even by something as tragic as death, our body's reaction is to let go and laugh.

My friend works in Intensive Care in a local hospital. She told me once how unnerved she was as a student the first time she was present when a doctor had to tell a man that his wife had died. She expected tears and screams, for the woman's death had been the result of an accident, quite sudden and unexpected. Instead, the man gave a short laugh, looked quite blank for a moment, then said, "Well, that's that," and walked out of the hospital. She recalls thinking how heartless he was. But time and experience and knowledge have showed her how really normal such a reaction is.

Emotional Overload

When we learn of the death of someone we love, more emotions than we can possibly handle come rushing forward, putting our emotional circuitry on overload. We cannot wonder, then, if the breakers snap over to "Off." In essence we are just protecting the entire system from burning out. When the overload lessens and it is safe to let the current run again, we will know it. And act on it.

Shock, this blessed absence of feeling, gets us through what must be done: the arrangements at the funeral parlor, the choosing of clothes for the body of our loved one, the wake and the unintentionally thoughtless things people tend to say at them, the funeral, the grave. From the outside we may appear very calm, very collected. We may even feel that way. But at some level of our beings, we are aware that this is only a respite.

We are, as it were, suspended between realities: the reality that was and the reality that is to be, the reality of life lived in company with the loved one and the reality of the rest of our earthly days deprived of that company. Shock is our psychological shield from the greatest and most immediate pain of our loss. It is the bridge over the most troubled of our waters. It is most assuredly a great gift from God.

Shock is generally accompanied by apathy and a degree of listlessness. We just simply don't care much about anything or anyone, even ourselves. We move like automatons through our days and nights, doing the minimum of what must be done—surviving. That is all. Oh, we dress and do our household work or go to the office. But nothing really penetrates the walls of our shock. Nothing really seems very important. We don't even care that we don't care.

Shock may last for moments or hours or days or months. It may leave and return later briefly and sporadically. To find ourselves back in the gray world of shock does not mean that our healing has stopped and will not be completed. It simply means that a greater pain than we can bear is emerging. Shock will get us through the worst of it.

How Can I Pray?

Does one, can one, pray in shock? Perhaps the rote prayers we all learned as children. If we care enough to pray at all, perhaps those. Certainly little, if anything more. I am reminded powerfully here of Jesus on the cross, surely in shock and crying out one of the remembered prayers from his childhood, a line from the psalms he must have memorized as all Jewish children did. "My God, my God, why have you forsaken me?" (Ps 22:1)

Do not be disturbed at your temporary inability to pray. Real prayer requires real feeling and in shock there is none. God understands. After all, he is the one who provided this beautiful numbness to get us through the agony. And he will wait, accepting as our prayer the feelings he knows are there even though temporarily we do not feel them.

Usually, but not always, shock does not last a very long time. The reality of death becomes present, the walls come tumbling down, and we begin the process of mourning in earnest. It is not pleasant and it is painful. It is also necessary. It is seeing our wound for what it is and allowing ourselves and God to probe it, clean it, perhaps stitch it, and certainly apply the balm of Gilead to it so that we may become healed and whole again.

Denial

Sometimes preceding shock, sometimes following it, sometimes nestled within it, is the phenomenon called denial. In denial, even though we *know* the loved one is dead, we refuse to accept it. We simply cannot face the actuality of death. We have seen the body, the coffin, and the grave; but our hearts refuse to put those images together in any meaningful pattern.

Some denial is normal. "No, it can't be true. It can't have

happened. She (or he) isn't dead. This is all a bad dream. When I wake up everything will be all right again."

This is the kind of magical thinking we embraced as children. If we wish something hard enough, it will be true. But we are adults now and so we allow reality to assert itself. After a short time of vehement denial, we accept the truth of what has happened and we go about the process of mourning.

But denial can become neurotic. For months, sometimes even years, we reject the actuality of death. This is not a "let's pretend" because even our use of the word "pretend" admits that what we are pretending isn't real. True denial is the concrete act of shutting out reality. We don't have to pretend death didn't happen because, in our denial, it didn't.

We speak of our loved one as alive. We set a place for him at table. We expect her at any moment to come through the door. We keep his or her room just as it was left, maybe even changing the sheets weekly so the bed will be fresh upon his or her returning. I even once had the bizarre experience of being invited to a birthday party for someone who had died nearly a year before! Thankfully, the party-giver went into therapy shortly thereafter and is now well and healed again.

People in extended, unhealthy denial have stopped mourning, have stepped out of the landscape of grief and into a fantasy land where the unreal has become real and the real does not exist. Their healing has been arrested. It cannot continue so long as they deny the need for it.

Neurotic denial cries out for professional help. If you are reading this book, you obviously are trying to cope with the reality of death. But perhaps you know someone who isn't.

Or perhaps someday you will. In my ministry as a spiritual director I recently came across a woman caught deeply in neurotic denial, and if it hadn't been for the powerful work of the Holy Spirit in us both, she might still be there. I'll call her Barbara.

Barbara's Perfect Family

Barbara first came to see me a little over a year ago. She is a woman in her late fifties and, though she presented herself as content, I was uneasy about something I couldn't name. She said she just wanted to get a little closer to God and felt a spiritual director might be the answer. She'd gotten my name from a friend.

As the weeks went by Barbara told me about her family: her "wonderful" husband Joe, her "perfect" son Allen, her "lovely" daughter Karen. As I listened to her stories, I was put more and more in mind of the television situation comedies of the late fifties, sort of an updated "Father Knows Best." But she did admit she had some trouble praying; though why, she couldn't imagine, since her life was really so happy and carefree.

We went on this way for a few months and my unease increased. I was seriously considering suggesting that she seek out someone else when our mutual miracle occurred. (There are those who would call it coincidence, though I can't help but think of a motto someone once told me: there are no coincidences, only miracles in which God chooses to remain anonymous.)

When Barbara arrived that particular day, I was under an unusual amount of stress. Besides the pressure of preparing to give a weekend retreat, that morning a good friend of mine had told me he had just found out he had AIDS, contracted sometime in the past before he had discovered the Lord in his life.

I apologized to Barbara for my distraction and mentioned that AIDS — up until then only a frightful word to me — had now become real because it was affecting someone I cared about. Barbara's reaction, or rather, overreaction amazed me. She nearly snarled and positively cursed the gay community. She ranted and raved and carried on and on. It was frightening to see this apparently gentle woman turn into an absolute Fury.

And suddenly I knew. God gave me the word and, thank God, I heard it. I waited for her to reach the end of her tirade, said a quick mental prayer for truth, and said, "Barbara, tell me about Allen."

She gasped, panted, looked wildly around the room, and burst into tears. And in that wonderful graced moment the story came out. Allen had died of AIDS two months before she ever came to see me. I trembled at what I had almost not seen. And I was humbled in the very real presence of Jesus in that small room as he broke gently through her denial and invited her mourning to begin.

Barbara and I are still companions on her healing journey. It's still a long way to the end. But the breakthrough happened. The denial shattered. And ultimately her healing will come.

Hopefully, this has helped to make clear the very real difference between shock and denial. Shock recognizes the reality while it protects us from the pain of it. Denial refuses to admit the reality at all. Both are natural and normal functions of the grieving process. It is only when either becomes protracted beyond a reasonable length of time (and this can vary from person to person) that it becomes neurotic and a stumbling block in our path to wholeness.

PRAYER

Lord God, I am empty.
I am in a desert place where there is nothing.
I cannot laugh. I cannot cry.
The sun comes up or goes down and I don't care.
I am so empty. I am nothing.
I have nothing. I care about nothing.

Be with me here.
I can't offer you anything but my being,
my breath,
the beating of my heart.
It is all I have.

I cannot feel your love
but help me to continue to believe that it is there.
Help me to believe that you are with me.
Help me to believe that I am still alive
and still one of your children.
Help me; for I cannot help myself.

Have pity on me, O Lord, for I am in distress;
with sorrow my eye is consumed;
my soul also, and my body.
For my life is spent with grief
and my years with sighing;
My strength has failed through affliction,
and my bones are consumed.
For all my foes I am an object of reproach,
a laughingstock to my neighbors,
and a dread to my friends;
they who see me abroad flee from me.
I am forgotten like the unremembered dead;
I am like a dish that is broken.
I hear the whispers of the crowd, that
frighten me from every side,
as they consult together against me...
But my trust is in you, O Lord;
I say, "You are my God."
In your hands is my destiny; rescue me from
the clutches of my enemies and my persecutors.
Let your face shine on your servant;
save me in your kindness.

PSALM 31

– 3 –

Disorientation and Disorganization

———— ♦ ————

> "And they all left him and fled. Now a young man followed him wearing nothing but a linen cloth. They seized him, but he left the cloth behind and ran off naked."
>
> (Mk 14:50–51)

And yet, if you had asked the apostles what they would do were Jesus arrested, running off into the night would not have been one of their answers. Doubtless they would have sworn to stand by him, to fight for him, even to die for him if need be. But desert him? Never!

Or think of Peter, huddled by the fire against the cold. The servant girl approaches. She looks at him closely and speaks.

> "You too were with Jesus of Nazareth." But he denied it saying: "I neither know or understand what you are talking about!" So he went out into the outer court. (Then a cock crowed.) The maid saw him, and began again to say to the bystanders, "This man is one of them." Once again he denied it. A little later the by-

> standers said to Peter once more, "Surely you are one of them; for you too are a Galilean." He began to curse, and to swear, "I do not know this man about whom you are talking!" (Mk 14:67–71)

> But Peter vehemently replied to Jesus, "Even if I have to die with you, I will not deny you." (Mk 14:31)

Strong emotion of any kind, be it fear, anger, grief, or even joy, can throw us into a state of disorientation and/or disorganization. And when that happens we act in strange ways, ways that are completely out of character, ways we cannot even attempt to predict. Fear caused this disorientation in the apostles, as it did in Jesus himself in the garden of Gethsemane.

> Then they came to a place named Gethsemane, and he said to his disciples, "Sit here while I pray." He took with him Peter, James, and John, and began to be troubled and distressed. Then he said to them, "My soul is sorrowful even to death. Remain here and keep watch." He advanced a little and fell to the ground and prayed that if it were possible the hour might pass by him; he said, "Abba, Father, all things are possible to you. Take this cup away from me, but not what I will but what you will." When he returned he found them asleep. He said to Peter, "Simon, are you asleep? Could you not keep watch for one hour? Watch and pray that you may not undergo the test. The spirit is willing but the flesh is weak." Withdrawing again, he prayed, saying the same thing. Then he returned once more and found them asleep, for they could not keep their eyes open and

> did not know what to answer him. He returned a third time and said to them, "Are you still sleeping and taking your rest? It is enough. The hour has come." (Mk 14:32–41)

To those who will take the time to envision this account, to put flesh and blood to Mark's terse reportorial style, a portrait of a very human, very frightened, very disorganized Jesus emerges. His former conviction about his mission is assailed by doubt. His heart is "filled with sorrow." He begs for a change in plan: "Take this cup away from me." According to Luke (22:44), "In his anguish... his sweat became like drops of blood falling to the ground." He keeps leaving his struggle with and in prayer with God to seek human consolation from his three best friends. He is short-tempered with his exhausted apostles, even with his good friend, Peter. Jesus is indeed in the grip of overpowering emotion, and it shows in his uncharacteristic and disoriented behavior.

Why have I gone to greater lengths here than elsewhere to show scriptural incidences of disorganization? Because this, more than any other phase of the mourning process, can be a danger zone for us. Not so much because of what we do or don't do, but because of the way disorganization and disorientation make us feel.

I make a distinction between disorientation and disorganization because my own experience of grief has shown me that while the two are concurrent, they affect me in different ways. Disorientation seems to grip my attitudinal processes, while disorganization is more clearly connected with behavior.

Disorientation

Disorientation makes us feel that we have lost our bearings, that in some way our former reference points have changed or are gone, which is certainly true following the death of someone close to us. Without ever being conscious of it, we frame our lives in great measure according to relationships. In many ways, we even define ourselves that same way.

I am wife, husband, mother, father, child, friend of . . . And I do this or that, act in a particular way, have certain expectations because of that relationship. And I know what is anticipated from me.

The sudden loss of one of these referents can put us for a while in the position of a sailor in the middle of an ocean whose compass has gone haywire on a cloudy night. We simply — and frighteningly — lose our sense of direction. To put it in terms with which we are probably more familiar, let me tell a very short, true story, that has happened to many of us at one point or another.

I grew up in Nashville, Tennessee, and knew that lovely city inside and out. It happened that after I became an adult I was away for several years. In that interim, the music industry moved in. Skyscrapers went up. Buildings were torn down or given false fronts. Recording studios were built. The tourist industry gave rise to countless little shops. Even some street names were changed. Then one day, I returned.

As I drove down Broad Street toward 21st I remember feeling as if I'd fallen down the rabbit hole or stepped through the looking glass. I mean, it was the same street, going the same way; but the landmarks were changed; the reference points were gone or altered. So, though I knew where I was, everything had become so different that I really wasn't certain of what I knew.

I pulled over and stopped the car, scanning the cityscape for some familiar thing to assure me that I really was where I thought I was. And I stayed there several minutes until I could reassure myself that though things looked very different the street was, in fact, the one I remembered and I was headed in the right direction.

Certainly, being "lost" in a familiar city is not so serious as being "lost" on our mourning journey. But the feeling is the same. And so is the panic. Nor is panic a state in which we would choose to live our lives. Pull your "car" over for a bit and be patient with yourself. Trust in God and your memory of your own good sense. In time the new becomes the familiar and you establish new bearings, new reference points, new relationships and ways of being.

Disorientation also usually includes a great deal of ambivalence in our attitudes, one of which a friend of mine calls "stay away closer." One of the great hazards of love is loss. We risk intimacy and when the other is torn away, the hole that is left cries out to be filled. We feel terribly isolated. We long for the full feeling of love. But, gripped by the fresh pain of our loss, we are afraid to risk again. So, though we yearn to be filled, we demand to be left alone. Which only increases our sense of isolation and our longing to be "with."

I think again of Jesus in the garden. He leaves most of the disciples behind, but asks Peter, James and John to come with him, to stay awake with him through his terrible agony. And yet, he leaves them behind too and insists on facing his night alone. When he returns and finds them asleep, he is angry that they have deserted him. He challenges them again to stay awake with him. But *again* he distances himself from them, and *again* they fall asleep.

"Stay away closer." The good news is that as we continue our healing journey, our ambivalence will fade away, our needs will become clearer, and we will be able to say to others, "Don't stay away. Come closer."

Disorganization

Disorganization tends more nearly to affect our behavior, both mental and physical. We may experience brief memory losses, an inability to concentrate or make decisions or work. Nightmares and/or insomnia may occur. The fact is that acute grief so disrupts the normal processes of the psyche that we do become dislocated and confused. And our bodies respond accordingly. We eat sparingly at meals and wake up ravenous in the middle of the night, bingeing wildly on the first thing that comes to hand and mouth. We can fall asleep at totally inappropriate moments but toss and turn endlessly at night. We drink too much, laugh too loudly, perhaps even flirt outrageously with a stranger. And we cannot understand what is causing this to happen.

We walk into a room and suddenly cannot recall why we are there. We make a phone call and, as we hear the ringing on the other end, we cannot remember who we are calling. Confirmed "neat-freaks" become sloppy and vice-versa. We do bizarre things for little or no apparent reason. One experience comes to mind.

The Red Dress

A friend of mine had just returned from burying her father. Her mother had died only a few months earlier. As the post-graveyard gathering went on downstairs, she called me up to her room. She was standing there in her slip, holding in her hand what I knew was the very expensive black dress she had worn to both funerals.

"I'm going to burn it," she laughed.

I knew it was futile to try to stop her. I could only attempt to minimize the danger to the house and to her as best I could. And I was able finally to convince her that the bathtub was a better place to set it afire than the middle of her bedroom. She put it in the bathtub, doused it with charcoal lighter, and set it ablaze, laughing wildly the whole time. Then she dressed in something completely flamboyant and at odds with the occasion (as I recall it was fire engine red and cut very low) and rejoined her friends.

Beware the Consequences

My friend's decision to burn her dress is a classic example of disorganization. It was strange and totally out of character, but happily it had no long-lasting effect on her life. What is unfortunate is that too often decisions are made during this time which do have far-reaching consequences. So it is important to realize the state we are in and try not to make any meaningful decisions.

This is not the time to sell the house, remarry, give away objects of sentimental value, throw out the family album, or change jobs. It is also not the time to burn your bridges, put the children into a new school, or tell the person who has always grated on your nerves just what you really think of him or her.

All these may seem to be very logical decisions, and in time they may be. BUT NOT NOW! You are in mid-ocean with a broken compass and the clouds are covering the stars. *Make no course changes.* They could be disastrous. Hard though it is, drift with the current. Wait for the sunrise to give you your bearings again.

Try, though it may seem to be against all reason, to do nothing but what must be done; and trust that Jesus will get you back into safe harbor. He will, but it takes time. And in the meantime, believe that he understands your confusion, your mistakes, your "craziness," your false starts and endless going in circles because he's been there. He knows.

Know the Danger

The greatest danger in this time of disorientation and disorganization is not, as I mentioned earlier, our behavior so much as it is the effect this behavior has on our self-esteem. We who have, in more normal times, been fairly confident of who we are and what we are doing, now find that we feel incompetent and unsure. We realize that we are off-center and we begin to wonder if we will ever be back on-center again. Has something unmendable broken within us?

We doubt ourselves, our ability to become loving, giving, functioning people again. Have we "lost it" for good?

We doubt others. How can they not see what we are going through? Have they just stopped caring? Did they ever really care at all?

We doubt God. After all, if God is such a loving parent, how can this be allowed to happen? Why is God letting me fall apart? Or is God even real?

In the midst of the confusion and turmoil, try to remember that what you are experiencing is normal and is temporary. You have not lost your mind. You are going to be okay.

May I use one more example from scripture to illustrate, to offer you hope in your distress?

> Now Saul, still breathing murderous threats against the disciples of the Lord, went to the high priest and asked him for letters to the synagogues in Damascus, that, if he should find any men or women who belonged to the Way, he might bring them back to Jerusalem in chains. On his journey, as he was nearing Damascus, a light from the sky suddenly flashed around him. He fell to the ground and heard a voice saying to him, "Saul, Saul, why are you persecuting me?" He said, "Who are you, sir?" The reply came, "I am Jesus, whom you are persecuting. Now get up and go into the city and you will be told what you must do." The men who were traveling with him stood speechless, for they heard the voice but could see no one. Saul got up from the ground, but when he opened his eyes he could see nothing; so they led him by the hand and brought him to Damascus. For three days he was unable to see, and he neither ate nor drank. (Acts 9:1–9)

Saul in this time of crisis certainly experienced all the symptoms of disorientation and disorganization. He fell to the ground, heard voices, even went blind in circumstances some would call emotional hysteria. He could not take any nourishment and he remained for a time in dark isolation.

But out of all this came the new Paul, a champion in the cause of Jesus Christ.

The ambiguity, the confusion, the sense of "blindness" are hard. We are not certain if and how we will emerge. But this sifting and resorting allows us to establish new landmarks. The very chaos makes space for new ways of ordering ourselves. Rather like a thorough spring cleaning, the disorder makes way for new patterns to emerge, patterns which help us in the new life direction we must necessarily undertake.

Be Patient

So again I urge you to be patient with yourself. Like shock, disorganization and disorientation, though to a degree painful in themselves, help to distract us from the greater pain and to get us through — in however haphazard a fashion — one of the most difficult times of mourning.

And know that God is strongly with you, aware of your situation and guarding you from hurting yourself and others whom you love. Feel his presence and allow him to help you.

PRAYER

God, I am confused.
Like St. Paul I seem to do what I don't want to do
and not to do what I wish to do.
I'm spinning, feeling out of control.
And I can't seem to help myself at all.
Why?
Why am I acting this way?

Help me, please. I feel so helpless.
I'm doubting myself in ways I've never doubted before.
And I'm wondering if I'll ever be me again.
Be with me in my confusion.

Be my rock in this tumbling world.
Be my strength.
For I have none of my own.

O Lord, my God, by day I cry out;
at night I clamor in your presence.
Let my prayer come before you;
incline your ear to my call for help.
For my soul is surfeited with troubles
and my life draws near to the nether world.
I am numbered with those who go down into the pit;
I am without strength.
My couch is among the dead...
My eyes have grown dim with affliction;
daily I call upon you, O Lord;
to you I stretch out my hands...
You have plunged me into the bottom of the pit,
into the dark abyss...
But I, O Lord, cry out to you;
with my prayer, I wait upon you.

PSALM 88

— 4 —

Sorrow

> When Jesus saw (Mary) weeping, and the Jews who had come with her weeping, he became perturbed and deeply troubled.
>
> (Jn 11:33)

When shock wears off, pain sets in. And that pain unlooses a host of emotions: sorrow, anger, relief, guilt. Feelings surface and are submerged only to surface again and again. Each is a different part of the landscape of grief, and each has its own mood, sound, color, and texture.

The often rapid coming and going of these emotions can leave us breathless and we find ourselves almost longing for the colorless barren plain of shock again. Difficult though this passage back and forth through strong, even violent, emotions can be, it too is a necessary part of the healing journey of mourning.

Back to the Locked Box

Most of us have a great deal of difficulty giving true expression to our emotions. Faithful to the Locked Box Syndrome which I mentioned in the Introduction, we have learned in ways obvious and subtle that real emotion makes people uncomfortable. Our need to be "in control" and the need of all around us to keep up the appearance of control have made our Locked Boxes full of unexpressed emotion a handy, if uncomfortable, way of life. We have confused civilization with repression; and we are paying a high price for that confusion.

Why does an extraverted expression of feeling seem to be too much? Why do we too often try to deny or lock up honest emotion? God gave us emotions for a reason. And saw that *everything* he had made was good. Are emotions an exception? I don't think so.

But I am afraid that the Locked Box is symptomatic of our age of high technology. Sentiment has been covered over with plastic and computer chips have replaced the "softer-ware" of the human heart. I would be the last to want to return to the time when housework was a twenty-four-hour-a-day job and plumbing was in the back yard. But, I fear, we are becoming too sleek, too programmed for our collective good.

The letting forth of real emotion must be recaptured if we are to be whole and healed people. For the person in mourning it is vital to the process. And yet, what does that person encounter?

"You're *relieved* it's over? Well... um... uh."

"Oh, you shouldn't be *angry* at him. After all, he's dead."

And the most damning and inhibiting of all: *"Don't cry."*

Why shouldn't we cry? Because it's messy and unattractive? Because people will stare? Because it makes others feel helpless and/or angry?

If you are in the grip of deep sorrow, the most normal natural thing you can do is cry. Tears are a great gift from God. They help to let the sorrow out and no one has the right to deprive you of that relief.

Oh, emotions are troublesome, all right, but denying or repressing them becomes even more troublesome.

Time Bombs

Unacknowledged, unexpressed emotions are time bombs. They can hurt us and others. They can make us spiritually ill. They can make us physically ill. They can make us psychologically ill. So it is vital to our healing that we let them out — all of them — and work and pray through them.

The only way to get through these feelings successfully is to acknowledge them, name them, and find your way to a resolution of them with the help of the Lord. This is the turning point in your grief though you may not feel it or realize it immediately. But it is the point at which Jesus can be a true consolation. For there is no emotion which Jesus himself did not experience. Therefore, there is no emotion which he cannot understand.

Are you sorrowful? So was Jesus. Are you angry? So was Jesus. Did he ever actually feel guilty? Of that we cannot be certain. But we can be certain that he assumed our guilt and that others tried to put guilt on him. And was there ever a more heartfelt cry of relief than when on the cross he called out, "It is finished"?

In his humanity Jesus felt all that we can feel. Now in his risen glory he only waits our word to help us with those feelings.

Remember, as you experience any or all of these emotions, that no feeling is bad or sinful. It simply is. You cannot help what you feel. You can only help what you choose to do about what you feel.

Sorrow

> "Where have you laid him?" he asked. They said to him, "Sir, come and see." And Jesus began to weep. (John 11:34–35)

Perhaps the first real feeling we have after the death of someone we love is profound sorrow. We cry, we moan. Our hearts quite literally hurt.

Part of our sorrow is genuinely for the one loved. Even those of us with deep faith wonder from time to time about life after death. Is there more? Is there joy now for this one whom I loved so much? Or has it all just simply ended? We need not be ashamed if we wonder. It is a part of our humanness. We are sorry too that the one who has died will miss some of the good things we expect to happen. "He would so much have loved to see this grandchild." Yes, certainly part of our sorrow is for the deceased.

But the greater sadness is for ourselves, for what we have lost and cannot have. It is a part of us that has been buried and we are deeply hurt that it cannot be reclaimed, recaptured. Death has cheated us of love, perhaps of security, and probably of our vision of long years ahead in the company of the one we loved. We weep for ourselves.

It is important to recognize that, to know that we are hurt, that losing someone does change our lives. For only then can we sorrow honestly and only then can healing take place.

I worked with someone once who kept saying, "Why am I sad? I believe my daughter is in heaven, and she's well and happy. So I shouldn't feel like this, should I? I shouldn't be so sad." It took time and prayer for her to realize that she was sad only in part because her *child* had died. The real sadness was for herself, that *she* had lost her child.

It's a subtle distinction but a necessary one. If her sorrow had never moved from what could not be changed (her daughter's death) to what could be changed (its function in her life), she could not have been healed.

As you sorrow, try to get in touch honestly with what your sorrow is really about. It is not selfish to mourn for yourself and that part of you now lost. If, God forbid, you ever had to endure the amputation of a limb, neither you nor anyone else would question your grief for yourself. No more need we feel wrong when the subject of a strong emotion is amputated from our lives. Especially when it is the overpowering emotion of love.

If you become a little or even a lot self-centered at this point, it is not because you are becoming mean and selfish. Part of you has died and, quite naturally, you are anxious to take extra care of what is left. Any "doing" for others may seem like much too great a risk. You are afraid to give away the little you feel you still have. Be patient with yourself. Your absorption in self will pass as you begin to tap the vast reservoirs of compassion and love which you will be surprised to find are still within you.

Sadness is painful, extremely so. But it's the emotion with which we are most comfortable in grieving because it is the emotion that is expected — by ourselves and by those around us. There are those who will say, "Don't cry." Ignore them. And there are those who will say, "It's okay to cry." Believe them. It is very okay to cry. For as long as you feel like crying, it is okay. Do it, and don't let anyone stop you. You are the one who is sorrowing. Only you will know when you've had enough.

PRAYER

Lord Jesus,
when you went to Lazarus' tomb you wept in sorrow.
You felt the pain of loss
so you know how heavy my heart is within me.
If you, who above all others
knew the joy of eternal life,
could weep,
then you understand my tears.

I don't ask you to take away the pain right away.
I know that it's part of saying good-bye.
But I do ask you to hold me close to you in my grief.
If I wish to weep with you,
I know you will understand.
And if you wish to weep with me,
I will feel the consolation of your love.

How long, O Lord? Will you utterly forget me?
How long will you hide your face from me?
How long shall I harbor sorrow in my soul,
grief in my heart day after day?
How long will my enemy triumph over me?
Look, answer me, O Lord, my God!
Give light to my eyes that I may not sleep in death
lest my enemy say, "I have overcome him."
Lest my foes rejoice at my downfall
though I trusted in your kindness.
Let my heart rejoice in your salvation;
let me sing of the Lord, "He has been good to me."

PSALM 13

— 5 —

Anger

> Since the Passover of the Jews was near, Jesus went up to Jerusalem. He found in the temple area those who sold oxen, sheep, and doves, as well as the money-changers seated there. He made a whip out of cords and drove them all out of the temple area, with the sheep and oxen, and spilled the coins of the money-changers and overturned their tables, and to those who sold doves he said, "Take these out of here, and stop making my Father's house a marketplace."
>
> (Jn 2:13–16)

Maybe you are more angry than sorrowing. Or maybe you are through (?) with sorrow and have moved into anger. You really feel angry, terribly angry.

But anger is not one of our "prettier" emotions. We were all taught, in fact, that anger is one of the Seven Deadly Sins. That is our image — and can be our undoing unless we can change the mentality that says good Christians don't get angry. To that I say, "Balderdash!" and several other less printable things. Anger is a feeling. Feelings are part of our human makeup. And God is the one who made us up. He gave us no more and no less than we need to be fully human.

Jesus, fully human as well as fully divine, got angry — and not just a little angry. He got *very* angry.

It's too bad that when scripture is read, it is usually done so in a relatively uninflected monotone. Why is a mystery, but I know I've heard better renditions of the Three Little Pigs than I've ever heard of the Gospels. Such reading tends to make Jesus sound pretty namby-pamby, even at some of his most emotional — and most angry — moments.

But think back to the angry Jesus, the one who called the Pharisees "hypocrites" and "blind fools," among other things (Mt 23:13–32); the one who drove the moneychangers out of the Temple — with a whip, no less (Jn 2:13–16); and the one who cried out on the cross, "My God, my God, why have you forsaken me?" (Mk 15:34). Think of how these words would be spoken, even screamed, if you were to say them. Then acknowledge that anger is acceptable. Get in touch with the angry Jesus who can help you face and honor and use your anger productively.

Being angry is not the opposite of loving. It is part of love, an important part. Surely Jesus loved the Pharisees, the moneychangers, his Father, even as he spoke out in anger. We speak of Jesus "cleansing" the temple, and that's a good image to keep. Anger *is* cleansing. The great energy released in anger can be like an enormous vacuum cleaner to our pain, sucking it out of every corner and leaving us clean.

In mourning the root of our anger is a sense of abandonment, of aloneness. We have been left behind, love torn violently from us. And we become, quite properly, angry.

The anger may be directed at the one who has died. How dare he do this to me? Couldn't she have lived longer if she'd really wanted to? That is a very normal reaction.

Despite our rational knowledge that the death was not

chosen (except in cases of suicide and even then we must wonder at the ability of the truly depressed to make a choice), our emotional level feels betrayed. We are the ones left behind to sort things out, to cope, to face all the problems and adjustments, to raise the children, to care for an aging parent, to make the mortgage payment. (I have a friend who was furious when her husband died because he had always been the one to get up early to make the coffee! While that may sound like a small thing, we cannot judge how important it might be to another.) Suddenly everything that was yours-plural has become yours-singular and yours *alone*. Your loved one has, in a sense, dumped everything into your finite lap and gone to the infinite God. Why not be angry?

Or the anger could be directed at others of your family. They were living closer, couldn't they see she was ill? If my brother hadn't broken my mother's heart by getting into drugs (or making a bad marriage or whatever) she'd be alive today! How could he have neglected her all these years?

When my father died, I was very angry: at him for not taking better care of himself, at my mother for not insisting he take better care of himself, at myself, at my brothers, my sister, my aunts, the priest who presided at the funeral, at everyone, or practically everyone, who came within my line of vision. Why? Because I could not face my real anger. I wouldn't even let it cross my conscious mind. Because the one I was really angriest at was the one I did not dare to be angry at. The truth was that I was angry with God.

"Why did my daddy have to die so young?" I wanted to scream in God's face. "Why did you do this? Why? I'd like to hurt you back. I'd like you to cry. I'd like to punish you in a thousand unnameable ways for taking my daddy away."

But, of course, I didn't scream that. I didn't even whisper it. Because to be angry at God, isn't that a sin? I'd go to hell if I did that, wouldn't I?

I no longer think so.

Jesus has taught me so many things since I decided to let him into my life, things about relationships and grief and hope and healing and pain. But more than anything else, he has taught me about love, the great and endless love of God for us, his wobbly children.

God knows how we feel. In giving us his son Jesus to be human as we are human, he closed the gap between Creator and creature. He is no longer God "out there" but Emmanuel, God with us. Jesus in his humanity learned all our joys and pains in a way so complete, so intimate that we need no longer fear to be intimate with God.

Yes, God knows how we feel. God is more able to take and transform our anger than anyone else. God understands. He watched, helpless, as his son's life was given up on the cross. And I can't believe that it didn't make him angry! Yet, what was his response? The resurrection and the good news that our sins have been forgiven. God is in our deepest heart and so he is in our deepest hurt. He is willing and able to accept our anger, to heal it if we just let go and express it.

Church Clothes

When we were children, we had what we called "church clothes." These were very special and, as the name implied, were worn *only* to church. They were nicer, prettier (or handsomer), more elaborate, more carefully starched and ironed than our everyday clothes. And these were what we wore when we went to God's house. After all, for a visit to God we had to look our very best: faces scrubbed pink, hair neatly combed into place, shoes sparkling, and clothes very elegant and very special.

Well, I suppose there was virtue in that if one really believes that cleanliness is next to godliness. What is most unfortunate, I think, is how such an attitude has carried over into our adult lives, most specifically into our adult prayer lives. So when we prepare to "pray," we clean it up. We scrub our words, shine up our thoughts, and very carefully dress up our prayers in their Sunday best. But to what purpose? So that God will think we are perfect?

In your heart you know that God knows everything. We have no secrets from him, though there are times when we wish we did. He knows we are angry. He knows we are angry at him. And that's okay. God can take it. He's bigger than our greatest anger. And he loves us enough, knows us enough, understands us enough to accept and transform that anger into power and energy for healing.

Reflect just a bit on Jesus and the children. Remember, the apostles tried to "shoo" them away. And why? Probably just because they were dirty and messy from playing all day. Children perennially have drippy noses, scabs on their knees, and knotted hair. They are rarely at their Sunday best. And they are naturally honest. Devastatingly so at times. But how did Jesus respond? Not only did he call them over, pick them up, and probably hug and kiss them, he told his followers that unless they were prepared to become just like little children, they could forget about finding the fullness of the kingdom of God (Mk 10:13–16). There is much in that little story to pray through.

Your Best Friend

Then, too, think about your best friend, the one you can have sit in your kitchen, wear curlers in front of, laugh with, cry with, be honest with, holler at, be angry at — and know that whatever passes between you will be understood because it is real communication between people who genuinely care about each other. And think what that relationship would become if every time you were going to meet that friend you put on your very best clothes and limited your conversation to how wonderful everything was. Probably very soon your friend would become nothing more than an acquaintance, and a distant one at that.

God wants to be your very best friend. He wants real communication to happen between the two of you. He loves your Sunday morning self. And he also loves your Thursday midnight self and your Saturday afternoon self and all the times and selves in between. So give him yourself, especially your anger. Let him have it! Really lay it on him. And don't be surprised if all he gives you in return is an overwhelming sense of love. You are not really alone after all.

Whatever you do with your anger, do anything but turn it in on yourself. Pray it, shout it, scream it, beat pillows, write it down. Do whatever you must to move it out from you. As long as you can get it out, you can deal with it and it cannot harm you. Left festering inside, it can make you ill, really ill. So move it out and let the healing touch of the Lord continue its good work in you.

PRAYER

(This is only intended to get you started on your angry prayer. Anger can be anything from ice-blue to fearsome red and I would not presume to try to put my anger into your wound. This is only a beginning. The rest is best said to God in your own words.)

Lord God,
I know that I am angry
and you know that I am angry.
But I am still a little afraid to say the words,
afraid you will not understand.
Please just give me enough faith in your love
that I may now speak honestly the things
that are troubling my heart.

Hearken, O God, to my prayer;
turn not away from my pleading;
give heed to me, and answer me.
I rock with grief, and am troubled
at the voice of the enemy and the
clamor of the wicked.
For they bring down evil upon me,
and with fury they persecute me.
Fear and trembling come upon me,
and horror overwhelms me,
And I say, "Had I but wings like a dove,
I would fly away and be at rest.
Far away I would flee;
I would lodge in the wilderness.
I would hasten to find shelter
from the violent storm and the tempest."
If an enemy had reviled me,
I could have borne it;
If those who hate me had vaunted themselves against me,
I might have hidden from them.
But you, my other self,
my companion and my bosom friend!...
But I will call upon God,
and the Lord will save me...
In the evening, and at dawn, and at noon,
I will grieve and moan,
and he will hear my voice.
He will give me freedom and peace.

PSALM 55

— 6 —

Relief

◆

> "It is finished." And bowing his head, he handed over the spirit.
>
> (Jn 19:30)

Frequently following the death of a loved one who has suffered a long and painful illness, there comes an undeniable sense of relief. The suffering is over. The sickness is ended. You know the person is beyond pain and is with God.

In those moments you can honestly and wholeheartedly thank God that death has given blessed ease to the suffering and has gathered the beloved to eternal rest in that place where there is no sickness or pain. That is a kind of relief which is no cause for trouble at all. We do not question it. Nor does it make us doubt our love.

But there is another sort of relief, also very common, especially if there has been a protracted illness before death. That is relief for ourselves. And we're liable to have almost as much difficulty with this as we have with being angry at God. Somehow, it just doesn't seem to be a feeling that we *should* have. It just does not seem very loving. Or very Christian.

Perhaps you're sitting over coffee after dinner and you find yourself thinking gratefully what a relief it is not to have to rush off to the hospital. Or you realize you are looking forward almost happily to a long Saturday with nothing in particular to do. Or you have a more general feeling of relief that your ordeal is past.

And what happens? You feel guilty! (See next chapter.) And, the truth is, there is no real reason to feel guilty at all, but you do feel it. The question becomes, how do you deal with it?

You have been through an awful time, a terrible time. And now it's over. Relief at such a moment is a true and honest feeling. Your life has not been normal at all during the illness. It's been rushed, often harried, constantly inconvenienced. Schedules have been totally thrown off. Leisure time has been non-existent. Life has been centered not around life but around approaching death. Granted, it was all for love. But it's still a terrible way to live. Now it's over. Can you really wonder that you are relieved?

And you've had to suffer the agonies of watching someone you love die. That's not a task any of us would choose. It is given to us and, in love, we accept it. But it entails tremendous suffering for us too. Now that is over. Relief is probably the most normal feeling to have.

There is one more kind of relief that it might help to be aware of: the relief when an abuser has died. I cannot go into the complex sets of feelings that exist in these relationships here, but I know from listening to people that great love frequently exists right alongside the fear. Which leads back again to the guilt trap when relief surfaces.

But try, for your own emotional health, to be at least a little objective in looking at the relief. When the one who has died has been an abuser — sexual, physical, or emotional — there is a great release for the survivors. As long as that person lived, you — or your children — were in actual danger.

Now the danger has gone. You are safe from having to face it again. The greatest love in the world would only be fooling itself if it did not admit to some sense of relief.

Feeling relief does not mean that you did not love. Nor does it render meaningless the life that you shared. It simply indicates that a burden has been lifted from you. Which is what the Lord wants for all of us. "Come to me, all you who labor and are heavily burdened, and I will give you rest" (Mt 11:28). That is Jesus speaking. Your burden has been lifted. In rest there is relief.

When I reflect on this particular aspect of the mourning journey, I cannot help but think of the faithful group beneath the cross: Mary, his mother; John, his beloved friend; and his Mary Magdalen. They had loved him so much. How their hearts must have ached to see his pain, his torment! And though they felt incredible sorrow as he died, there must have been relief too when it was finally over.

The Pieta comes into my mind. The heartbroken mother holding the broken son. Could she have not, through her tears, felt relief that both he and she had come to the end of that particular agony?

PRAYER

Holy Mother Mary,
as you watched your son die,
how you must have prayed that it would end
—for him—and for yourself.
And when it finally did,
a part of you must have been relieved
that his suffering and yours were over.

Help me now to accept my relief
as a normal human emotion
and do not let it turn back in on me as guilt.
Ask your son to stay with me in this time
and to console me with his humanity and yours.

Have mercy on me, O God, in your goodness;
in the greatness of your compassion wipe out my offense.
Thoroughly wash me from my guilt
and of my sin cleanse me.

Cleanse me of sin with hyssop, that I may be purified;
wash me, and I shall be whiter than snow.
Let me hear the sounds of joy and gladness;
the bones you have crushed shall rejoice.
Turn away your face from my sins,
and blot out all my guilt.

A clean heart create for me, O God,
and a steadfast spirit renew within me.
Cast me not out from your presence,
and your holy spirit take not from me.
Give me back the joy of your salvation,
and a willing spirit sustain in me.

I will teach transgressors your ways,
and sinners shall return to you.
Free me from blood guilt, O God, my saving God;
then my tongue shall revel in your justice.
O Lord, open my lips,
and my mouth shall proclaim your praise.

PSALM 51

— 7 —

Guilt

When Jesus returned to Capernaum after some days, it became known that he was at home. Many gathered together so that there was no longer room for them, not even around the door, and he preached the word to them. They came bringing to him a paralytic carried by four men. Unable to get near Jesus because of the crowd, they opened up the roof above him. After they had broken through, they let down the mat on which the paralytic was lying. When Jesus saw their faith, he said to the paralytic, "Child, your sins are forgiven." Now some of the scribes were sitting there asking themselves, "Why does this man speak that way? He is blaspheming. Who but God alone can forgive sins?" Jesus immediately knew in his mind what they were thinking to themselves, so he said, "Why are you thinking such things in your hearts? Which is easier, to say to the paralytic, 'Your sins are forgiven,' or to say, 'Rise, pick up your mat and walk?' But that you may know that the Son of Man has authority to forgive sins on earth" — he said to the paralytic, "I say to you, rise, pick up your mat, and go home." He rose, picked up his mat at once, and went away in the sight of everyone.

> They were all astounded and glorified God, saying, "We have never seen anything like this."
>
> (Mk 2:1–12)

I always think of this story when I think of guilt because guilt so often keeps us on our mats, paralyzed and turned inward. Guilt is in a category by itself for it is the most paralyzing of all the emotions we may experience following the death of someone we love. And it seems to be universal.

There is guilt for things we did, guilt for things we didn't do, guilt others can lay upon us, justified guilt, unjustified guilt and even, sometimes, guilt that *we* are still alive!

A very dear friend of mine once opened a marvelous door for me when he said that guilt — except for the honest and healthy expression of regret for sin — does not come from God. And he is absolutely right. God wants freedom for us, the freedom to enjoy this wonderful playground we call creation. Guilt is anything but freedom. It is a prison. Worse, it is total paralysis.

If Only

"If only I had..." "If only I hadn't..." We tote up all the big and little commissions and omissions in which we feel we have failed in a relationship. We feel terrible and terribly guilty. And we become just as paralyzed by our sins real and imagined — as was the paralyzed man at Capernaum.

Some regret for our inadequacies can be a cause for growth as a person. "Live and learn," as it were. And "learn" is the operative word. We all sin; we all make mistakes; we all have moments in our lives we wish we could relive differently.

That is part of being human. But we can learn from those experiences. We can discover our weaknesses in them and pray for healing of those weaknesses.

I am reminded of part of the "confession formula" I learned as a child: "I firmly resolve with the help of your grace to confess my sins, to do penance and to *amend my life.*"

By placing our weaknesses in the loving atmosphere of God's grace, we are enabled to amend our lives, to do better, to avoid repeating our mistakes, and so to live holier lives. That also is part of being human. But it can only happen when we let go of our guilt, that awful paralysis that holds us fast to our mats and refuses to allow us to walk.

Perhaps we could replace those "if only's" with a slightly different one to help get things into perspective. Try instead, "If only I had known." Yes, if only you *had* known that was going to be your last word to him or her, your last Christmas together, your last smile, your last anything, it might have been different. If only you had known. But you didn't. You didn't know. And that's the place where truth and freedom can begin for you. *You didn't know.*

Even in cases of long illness, no one knows the exact day or hour when death will occur. In fact, frequently we are fooled by a brief rallying on the part of the one dying. That is not an uncommon phenomenon. Many times shortly before death, the loved one seems to be getting better. And we, in our love, want so desperately to believe it is true that we do believe it. Then death comes and we are left bewildered. If only.... No. Not, if only. If only you had known.

If the death were unexpected—an accident, a sudden heart attack, a suicide—we couldn't even have guessed. But, oh, how the unhappy memories taunt us.

I'm going to share something with you now that I've never told anyone before. At first I felt too guilty to tell anyone and I clutched that guilt to myself for a long, long time. Later, when the good God helped me see it for what it was and took it gently away, it seemed pointless to mention it. But now, as you and I and the Lord are working together to ease your guilt, it may be that the time for my story has come.

The Last Time I Saw My Father

The last time I saw my father alive was at the Nashville airport. I was on my way back to New Jersey after a trip home to visit, and the whole family came out to see me off. Well, the plane was delayed as planes are wont to be and we hung around the boarding area making the kind of idle conversation people make when they know they can be interrupted at any minute.

Except that in my family there is very little that doesn't become intense—rapidly. As a result, my father and I had some sort of disagreement. I no longer have any recollection what it was about. It could have been politics. It could have been the weather. It could have been how many angels will fit on the head of a pin! But when my flight was called we were still in the heated midst of it and our leavetaking was not as loving as usual.

Less than a month later he was dead of a heart attack. And for years, weaving in and out of my life like some terrible dirge, the only image I could conjure of me and my much loved daddy was that final scene at the airport. "If only I hadn't insisted." "If only I'd said he was right." "If only I'd told him I loved him." If only. If only. Until one night when the scene was replaying for the thousandth time in my head, I cried, "If only I'd known!"

And at that moment God moved in. If only I'd known. But I didn't. I couldn't have. And suddenly dozens of happier memories emerged and I was freed from my mat of guilt.

"If only I had known." That is the key to ridding yourself of guilt, because all you can ever be is who you are at any given moment. You react, respond out of your own awareness at that time, your own perfectly imperfect human awareness. And that's all you can be responsible for. So if your last moments with your loved one were less than completely loving, so be it. *You did not know.* You did not plan it that way. You did not know they were going to be the last.

Guilt doesn't only hide in momentous things like last words, however. It can hide in a thousand memories, poisoning them and you with bitterness. Don't let it. Keep reminding yourself that the "you" who is reading this page is not the "you" who existed yesterday, or even the "you" who existed before you ever picked up this book. Much less is it the "you" of a year or five years or ten years ago. So the "you" of today must not insist on carrying the guilt of all those former "you's" who no longer exist. To do so is to allow the paralysis to keep you helpless on your mat of guilt.

Give Your Pain To Jesus

Invite Jesus into your painful memories and ask him to be there with you. Let him walk with you on your own road to Emmaus (Lk 24:13–35). Remember how he joined the two who walked there and asked them to share their memories with him? He listened and then interpreted for them what they remembered and had heard but not understood. The result was that they were healed. Jesus took them from being "in distress" to feeling their "hearts burning" with love and understanding.

Jesus is no less ready to journey with you into your painful memories. Invite him in, let him be with you and with whomever else was present, listen with the Lord's ears to what was said, and let him speak to your hurting heart. By consciously sharing this time with him you allow him to touch the hurt place and make it well again. Though you cannot change what has happened, you can let the Lord change how you feel about it.

Call up memories of good times, happy times; and enjoy those whenever guilt tries to hold you prisoner again. Jesus spent his ministry freeing people from their guilt, teaching and living forgiveness. "And forgive us our trespasses as we forgive those who trespass against us." As we forgive others, let us also forgive ourselves. Clinging to guilt forbids forgiveness, binds us to our mats, and refuses to let us walk in freedom.

There is another kind of guilt we need to be aware of: that is the guilt that comes from *outside.* And it comes from those from whom we would least expect it, others who are sharing our grief. It is their own sorrow and anger which gives rise to it, and we can all too easily become the victims. They accuse us — usually without actually meaning to — in so many ways and we are stunned. Unfortunately and all too often, we appropriate their statements and add them to our guilt. But again, Jesus shows the way to healing. Consider this.

> Martha said to Jesus, "Lord, if [only] you had been here, my brother would not have died." . . . When Mary came to where Jesus was, and saw him, she fell at his feet and said to him, "Lord, if [only] you had been here, my brother would not have died." (Jn 11:21, 32)

While I'm certain that neither Mary nor Martha intended to heap guilt on Jesus, consider the effect their remarks could have had. Think how you might feel if someone said such a thing to you. Would you be angry? Would you incorporate that guilt into yourself? But look at Jesus here. He neither reproved nor reproached them. Most certainly he did not take guilt upon himself. Instead he went on to the tomb, had the stone rolled away, and called Lazarus forth.

When others attempt to pile "if only's" upon us, we too can roll away the stone and call forth our own innocence, our happy recollections, the sure knowledge of our love. In doing so we can drop the winding sheets of guilt. Both we and our loved ones can be unbound as Jesus commands. "Untie him," Jesus told them, "and let him go free" (Jn 11:44).

And so we are freed from guilt and memories that sting. It is not the wish of the Lord Jesus that we be paralyzed or bound up in winding sheets. It is not the wish of our prodigal Father that we live out our lives doing penance for what is past. And it is not the wish of the Holy Spirit, the Giver of Life, that we refuse that life to hold on to the deadliness of guilt.

I would like to close this section with a story that seems to me in a lovely way to help put closure on our guilt once and for all.

The Lady and the Bishop

Once upon a time there lived a very holy lady. Desiring to have much solitude with God she went to live as a hermit in a cave in the mountains. But, of course, the people from her village knew about her and slowly but surely word spread of this very holy woman.

It followed then that people looking for spiritual consolation came to her cave to visit her, and she prayed with them and shared unselfishly all that she had come to know about the Lord. More and more people came and inevitably word of this extraordinary woman reached the ears of the local Bishop. Naturally he was concerned for his people and wanted to be certain of the lady's orthodoxy and authenticity. So he sent for her.

So she came down to the city and knocked at the door of the Bishop's palace. He was quite cordial to her and led her to a table where a sumptuous meal was served. But over dessert, he got serious, even stern.

"I'm told," he said, "that you live as a hermit and that many people come to you for spiritual guidance."

"That's true, your Excellency," she said.

"You give them spiritual counsel? But where did you study theology? Where did you learn spirituality? Where did you get your degrees?"

"Oh, I'm sorry, your Excellency, but I haven't any. I only finished high school, nothing more."

"And yet you dare to offer spiritual advice?"

"Only as the Lord directs me, sir."

"I see. I'm also told that you claim God speaks to you."

A lovely light passed over her face. "Oh, yes, your Excellency. He does!"

"God *speaks* to *you?*"

"Yes, sir, he does."

"Well then, do me a favor. The next time you and God are talking, ask him to tell you what *my* sins are."

"If that be your wish, sir."

"Make sure he knows that it's *my* sins you want to know. Then report back to me."

With that the lady left and walked back happily, if somewhat puzzled, to her cave.

A few months went by and the lady's reputation only continued to grow. Even people from outside the vicinity were making their ways to the cave in the mountains. But still the bishop heard nothing from her. Nettled, he sent for her again.

This time when she arrived there was no table laid. Instead, the bishop in the full regalia of his office met her very formally and ushered her into his conference room.

"I expected to hear from you before this," he said. "Tell me, have you spoken to God again?"

"Yes, your Excellency."

"And, I suppose, you asked him to tell you my sins?"

She nodded again.

"You asked him quite specifically for a list of my sins?"

Another nod.

"And, tell me, what did God say to you?"

"He told me to tell you, sir, that he's forgiven all your sins and so he's sorry he can't give me the list because, quite frankly, he's forgotten them."

If that be God's attitude, can we not try to make it our own as well?

PRAYER

Jesus, heal me.
I am as paralyzed as anyone you ever cured in Israel
and I need you.
Guilt for all the times I failed to be loving
has me bound here, helpless.
I want to walk again.
I want to live a whole life.

But I am tormented by the past.
My soul moans in regret.
I cannot seem to remove this awful burden.
Please, take it from me, Jesus,
and let me walk with you in peace.

My God, my God, why have you forsaken me,
far from my prayer, from the words of my cry?
O my God, I cry out by day, and you answer not;
by night, and there is no relief for me . . .
Be not far from me, for I am in distress;
be near, for I have no one to help me . . .
I am like water poured out;
all my bones are racked.
My heart has become like wax
melting away within my bosom.
My throat is dried up like baked clay,
my tongue cleaves to my jaws;
to the dust of death you have brought me down. . . .
But you, O Lord, be not far from me;
O my help, hasten to aid me.
Rescue my soul from the sword,
my loneliness from the grip of the dog.
Save me from the lion's mouth;
from the horns of the wild bulls, my wretched life.

PSALM 22

— 8 —

Loss and Loneliness

♦

> She thought it was the gardener and said to him, "Sir, if you carried him away, tell me where you laid him, and I will take him." Jesus said to her, "Mary!" She turned and said to him in Hebrew, "Rabbouni," which means Teacher. Jesus said to her, "Stop holding on to me, for I have not yet ascended to the Father. But go to my brothers and tell them, 'I am going to my Father and your Father, to my God and your God.'" Mary of Magdala went and announced to the disciples, "I have seen the Lord," and what he told her.
>
> (Jn 20:11–15)

The full awareness of loss and the accompanying loneliness can be devastating. Suddenly, as Edna St. Vincent Millay said, "The presence of that absence is everywhere." No matter where you are, who you are with, or what you are doing, you are painfully aware of feeling alone.

The loss has been a physical one, yes. But it is also an emotional and a spiritual one. We are deprived of an intimacy that we had come to count on, and our sense of isolation is overwhelming.

Many turn to a sort of human hibernation at this point, sitting alone and refusing invitations, refusing even to answer the telephone or open their mail. They act out exactly what they are feeling. This is a time of real darkness. God seems to be gone and you are left suffering and alone. You are very much in the position of the weeping Magdalene at the tomb.

You are afraid to "reconnect" with the world, to risk any intimacy, to reach out. After all, death is a reality and it is everywhere. What if it happens again? So you choose isolation as a defense. What you do not have, you cannot lose. If you do not love, you cannot be hurt. And so you sit — alone.

Be very gentle with yourself right now. The hope I give to you is that this time of acute loneliness can be the final signpost on your travel through mourning. Hard though it may be to believe and no matter how often it has been said before, this onset of darkness usually presages the dawn. If you allow this last terrible pain to be felt and deal with it, you are well on the way to the healing that both you and the Lord desire. Though at the moment you probably feel that healing is farther from you now than it ever was, take heart. Your deep grief is probably coming to an end.

A Friend

At this time, right now — more than any other — you need a friend.

Oh, I imagine that's the last thing you think you want. Conversation is an effort, too much of an effort. You really just want to be alone. But talking about your feelings, your loved one, your sense of loss and loneliness can help you get through the darkness safely and more quickly. Ah, you think, but who wants to listen? Who wants to enter into this grief with me?

My response to you is: any loving friend. Remember? The one you don't have to dress up for? The one who'd rather have coffee in your kitchen than high tea in the living room? Somewhere among your friends and family is someone who is willing, even anxious not to abandon you in this time of need.

> "Go back, my daughters!" said Naomi. "Why should you come with me? . . . No, my daughters, my lot is too bitter for you, because the Lord has extended his hand against me. . . . " But Ruth said, "Do not ask me to abandon or forsake you! for wherever you go I will go, wherever you lodge, I will lodge, your people shall be my people, and your God my God." (Ru 1:11, 13, 16)

Be certain that God has provided each of us with a Ruth, someone who will be with us no matter what or where or how. Listen to her, talk with her, and let her into your loneliness. She will be a steadfast companion, willing to weep when you weep and rejoicing when you are healed.

To shut ourselves off from friendship now can be one of the most serious errors we can make. It is easy for the grieving one to say no to friendship and to insist on isolation. But what tragedy can result. Instead of taking this last, albeit difficult, leg of your journey, the griever sinks to the ground, unable to finish the walk alone and unwilling to ask for help. Then genuine clinical depression can take over, and often does. If this happens professional help will probably be needed before the mourning process can be ended.

There are other tragedies that occur at this time. People have turned to drugs and alcohol for relief rather than to a friend and God. Drugs and alcohol don't help, not really. They may provide a temporary numbness but all they actually do is stop the necessary grieving process. Sooner or later, the aching resurfaces and must be dealt with if you are to go on to your own personal living resurrection.

Try to remember that God is there even though you can neither see nor feel him. Just as Mary Magdalene at the tomb could not recognize her Lord in the blindness of her tears of loss, so we often cannot recognize him in the guises in which he may come before us. A loving friend can be Jesus for us if only we allow it.

PRAYER

God, are you anywhere?
If you "are" at all, why aren't you here?
I am so alone in this darkness.
Why have you left me?

I feel weak.
I hardly have the strength left to breathe.
Even saying this prayer is too much of an effort.

If you're there, come to me.
Be with me.
Be ***with*** *me.*
I am alone.
And I am frightened.

Out of the depths I cry to you, O Lord;
Lord, hear my voice!
Let your ears be attentive
to my voice in supplication:

If you, O Lord mark iniquities,
Lord, who can stand?
But with you is forgiveness,
that you may be revered.

I trust in the Lord;
my soul trusts in his word.
My soul waits for the Lord
more than sentinels wait for the dawn.

More than sentinels wait for the dawn,
let Israel wait for the Lord,
For with the Lord is kindness
and with him is plenteous redemption;
And he will redeem Israel
from all their iniquities.

PSALM 130

— 9 —

After a Suicide

♦

Father, into your hands I commend my spirit.
(Lk 23:46)

The death of a loved one is always difficult. But it is particularly awful when the death was by suicide. There is such anger and despair in the act itself, that we quite literally feel assaulted, shoved over a precipice from which there is no rescue. The wind rushes wildly past us and we feel this violent descent has only one possible ending: our own death.

All the symptoms of mourning which we have discussed in this book will be present, but intensified. None more so than our enemy guilt. And to that may be added a great burden of shame and anger.

David

What I will attempt to do now is to share, out of my experience as a friend of one who completed suicide, some realizations I came to, not alone, but with the help of others and always in company with my God.

The first came when the initial shock wore off and I realized that I was furious with myself and also with the people who lived with David. (David is not really his name, but calling him "my friend" over and over again begins to grate on the ear and tends to distance him from me in a way I don't like.)

The thought of our long distance phone call tormented me (see page 24). What had I missed? What had I not said? Why had I not caught the next plane and gone to see him? What sort of friend was I?

And what about his house-mates? his psychiatrist? They were right there! How could they have been so stupid? How could they have let him be so sad, so isolated? Why hadn't we realized just how depressed David was? There had been signs, clues. We all "should" have seen them.

But, I learned, predicting suicide is never completely accurate — until it has happened. Only then does our hindsight become certainty. Only then can we really know.

In truth, all had been done for David that could have been done without tying him up in a bare, locked room. Much as I might have wanted to, I could not have gone to see him right at the time he called. Nor could his housemates have been more caring and concerned. We had done as much as we could. Beyond that there was nothing to be done.

My anger, I discovered, was the child of my pride. And as I began to understand and believe that, I managed to forgive all of us, even David.

Realization two came after I moved into extreme guilt. If I'd only been with him, it wouldn't have happened. The truth is that once someone has *decided* to take his or her own life, nothing and no one can stop them. Even in a hospital. I could have been at David's side every moment, and he still could have found a way to complete his death. The person truly intent on suicide cannot be stopped.

The third step in my healing came when I realized and acknowledged that the only life I am completely responsible for is my own. If it were my choice, had it been my decision, David would be alive today. But my responsibility toward him was to love him, to reach out to him, to let him know how valuable he was to me. Those things I did. And there my actual responsibility ceased. I can't say that realization immediately ended my guilt. I felt like a failure as a friend. But with prayer and the help of my spiritual director, I finally came to believe that David and only David was responsible for his life — and his death.

The "Stigma" of Suicide

Unfortunately our culture has too often operated out of a confused belief system, making us heir to a certain degree of shame about suicide. Thank God, I was spared that. Modern psychology has enlightened us on many fronts and this is one of them.

Unhappily, though, many people still do attach a stigma to suicide. They feel it is a disgrace, a dishonor. The fact is that it is no more a disgrace than death from any other illness. It is tragic, yes, but it is not shameful.

For the sake of your own healing, confront the word "suicide," don't deny it. Allow the Lord to show you that it is only another word, no better or worse than a thousand others. And pray for the grace not to allow the mistaken attitudes of others to affect your own behavior.

Why?

Why did he do it? Why did a young, handsome, sensitive, religious man whose life's ministry seemed to stretch out in lovely patterns before him choose to complete suicide? I had some clues, I had some guesses. But I had no concrete answer. Why? It is an inevitable question we ask when faced with the suicide of someone we love. And it probably has no answer in this life. But ask it, struggle with it even. There can be learning here. Then let it go. To continue to torment yourself endlessly with an unanswerable question serves no good purpose and only stops your mourning journey.

And cling fiercely to God. Know that he is with you and wants to comfort you. Know that your loved one is with him. I had no difficulty believing that David was with God. A God who loves us as passionately as our God does surely has compassion on those so bruised and torn that they can no longer cope with life.

A Final Reflection

There is one final reflection I had which I pray will help you. I do not believe that David's death was "God's will." I do not believe that God ever wills sickness, pain, and suffering for his children any more than any loving parent would ever will such things for a child. How could a God who loved enough to send Jesus ever wish us evil? I don't believe he does.

I do believe that David's decision to complete suicide was a working of the imperfect human condition.

But time after time, I have found that — when we allow it — God can and will bring good out of even the worst of our human messes. Very shortly, I discovered that for me the suicide of David was no exception.

I was just emerging from my grief over David, just beginning to feel freedom from that pain, when a member of my own family attempted, but did not complete, suicide. I was tossed head over heels back into the blackness of sorrow, of guilt and anger and confusion. How could this happen again?

But the blackness was different this time — because David was there with me. I could feel his presence as surely as if I could have seen him. And in my misery I prayed to him to intercede on my family's behalf, to present our sorrow first hand to the Lord and ask him to ease it.

I believe he did that very thing, for as I prayed I felt my sorrow ease.

And that was the blessing, that I had David who understood better than any of the rest of us what my family member was going through, David who could pray for us in the very face of God.

PRAYER

Oh God, I feel like such a failure.
And I keep asking myself
how this could have happened,
and why?
Oh, the endless why.

Where did I fail?
Did I love enough?
too much?
Will this terrible pain ever go away?

Help me, God,
to accept what I cannot understand.
Give me your peace and a quiet heart.
Oh God, how I need peace.

Hear, O Lord, the sound of my call;
have pity on me, and answer me.
Of you my heart speaks; you my glance seeks;
your presence, O Lord, I seek.
Hide not your face from me;
do not in anger repel your servant.
You are my helper; cast me not off;
forsake me not, O God my savior.
Though my father and mother forsake me,
yet will the Lord receive me.

PSALM 27B

— 10 —

The Death of a Child Before Birth

Rise up, shrill in the night,
at the beginning of every watch;
Pour out your hearts like water
in the presence of the Lord;
Lift up your hands to God
for the lives of your little ones.

(Lam 2:19)

Any death of a loved one is heart-breaking. But the death of a child must be the worst. And when that death comes before the child ever experiences life outside the womb, the death is not only tragic but seems incomplete somehow. The grief it leaves behind can be devastating.

If your child miscarried or was stillborn, my heart goes out to you. I can't pretend to "understand" because it is a suffering I have never endured. But I know it is real. I know it is hard. I also know it can be healed.

All of what has already been said here about grieving applies, all the emotions, all the loss and loneliness. It's important for you to know that, and even to be selfish about it if you must. Our society tends to gloss over a miscarriage as "just one of those things"; but if you are the parent and the baby was yours, it is not. You are unique. Your child was unique. You have the need — and the right — to grieve.

Take all the time you need. "Snapping out of it," as you will undoubtedly be urged to do, will not cure you, will not heal you. Only time, the comfort of your spouse or best friend, and the great love of God will bring you back to peace. Take time. Be gentle with yourself. Allow your heart to mend.

Your emotions are going to run the gamut as discussed in Chapter 4. So we need not go over them again. But be alert especially to two of the most powerful emotions you may be feeling: guilt and fear.

Guilt and Fear

That your child died so soon is *not* your fault. You did nothing wrong. Why children miscarry, why they die in the womb is often a mystery. You know how happy you were, how carefully you treated yourself. You know the songs your heart sang to your baby. You are not to blame. Refuse the guilt. It cannot help you. Give it to Jesus and ask him to take it away.

Many parents who have suffered the death of a child before its birth are also fearful of another pregnancy. It's a normal and a natural fear. Allow it to be, if it must; but as your healing continues, let that wound be closed as well. Most probably at some time you will have a complete pregnancy and the great delight of holding a baby in your arms. As God says to us in Isaiah 43 and 44, "Fear not . . . I will pour out my spirit upon your offspring, and my blessing upon your descendants. They shall spring up amid the verdure like poplars beside the flowing waters." That is God's promise to us, to you. Fear not; and, when the time comes, move confidently into your future.

Your Special Needs

As a grieving parent you have some very special needs for — in many ways — you will be exposed to some well-intentioned but painful remarks, made in the name of comfort but falling far short of it.

First of all, try to ignore and forgive all your well-meaning friends who might tell you that it's probably "all for the best," that miscarriages are nature's way of "taking care" of something gone wrong, that it is "God's will," that what you *should* do is "get pregnant again right away," as if it were easy to substitute one child for another.

It doesn't matter really if your friends are right or wrong. What matters are your feelings. And I doubt that you feel that the loss of your child was for the best. Do try to understand, however, that those friends are really trying to help you through a very difficult time. Their intentions are good even if their words are hurtful to you.

Nor do I believe that the loss of your child was "God's will." As I've said before, I don't believe, for an instant, in a God who wills pain and suffering. Every act of Jesus on earth — Jesus, who did nothing but the will of God — was an act of love and healing. God did not, does not will that you should suffer.

God is our parent, our mother, our father, who gives birth to everything that is and who understands in a way we can't even begin to imagine what it is to suffer the death of a child.

We are God's children and our children are also, the born and the unborn. None of us escapes divine notice, infinite love.

> Can a mother forget her infant,
> be without tenderness for the child of her womb?
> Even should she forget,
> I will never forget you.
>
> (Is 49:15)

God Shares Your Pain

The loss you feel now is God's loss also. God, mother and father, knows your pain. "It was now about noon and darkness came over the whole land until three in the afternoon because of an eclipse of the sun. The veil of the temple was torn down the middle. Jesus cried out in a loud voice, "Father, into your hands I commend my spirit"; and when he had said this he breathed his last" (Lk 23:44–46). I've often prayed this scripture and I've come to believe that the eclipse and the rending of the temple curtain were expressions of God's incredible pain at the death of Jesus. In those awful moments, God's sadness darkened the earth. God's anger struck out at the Holy of Holies in retribution for what had been done to the Holiest One of all. Yes, God understands your grief; it has been his grief as well.

Our God is, above all, a compassionate God, a God who stands with us and among us and who suffers as we suffer. God's love for us is neither abstract nor cerebral. It is as real as the love you feel for your child. "But now, thus says the Lord, who created you . . . and formed you . . . : Fear not, for I have redeemed you; I have called you by name; you are mine"

(Is 43:1). God's love embraces you and wants to heal you. Let God, father and mother, love you back to wholeness.

Commend Your Child To God

Many bereaved parents whom I have counseled have found peace in visioning their child in heaven. So healing has this been that I urge you to do the same, to name your baby, and to have Mass celebrated in the baby's memory. Your child no longer has need of your prayers, but you do. A Mass will bring you into deeper and more intimate contact with Jesus our Healer and will bring you some comfort as you formally commend your child into the care of God. Let this word of God bring you comfort.

> Farewell, my children, farewell:
> I am left desolate.
> I have taken off the garments of peace,
> have put on sackcloth for my prayer of supplication...
> With mourning and lament, I sent you forth,
> but God will give you back to me
> with enduring gladness and joy.
>
> (Bar 4:20 and 23)

God *will* give your child back to you in time, for your child has now been welcomed into heaven and beholds the very face of Love. Your baby is happy and whole and healed... and now prays for you among the angels.

Feel your child in heaven, beyond suffering and pain, laughing and happy. You might even want to imagine him or her in the care of that best of all human mothers, Mary, just waiting for the day when you will be reunited in a place of unending joy.

And Be Comforted

Allow Jesus to comfort you. Allow yourself to be healed of this great grief. God is with you. Your child is with you. Move gently through this time of sadness. Move gently and be healed.

PRAYER

Lord Jesus,
you loved little children
even when they were hot and dirty from playing
and your apostles wanted to "shoo" them away.
It helps me to know that
and to believe that now you and your mother
are caring for my child.

But, Jesus,
my arms are empty and my heart is broken.
So many hopes, so many plans and dreams
have been taken.
I need you too; I need you now.
Oh, Jesus, how I need!

Touch me, Lord.
Touch the empty place within me
where my baby took life.
Touch and heal me, Jesus,
for I cannot bear this alone.

When the Lord brought back the captives of Zion,
we were like people dreaming.
Then our mouth was filled with laughter,
and our tongue with rejoicing.
Then they said among the nations,
"The Lord has done great things for them."
The Lord has done great things for us;
we are glad indeed. Restore our fortunes, O Lord,
like the torrents in the southern desert.
Those that sow in tears
shall reap rejoicing.
Although they go forth weeping, carrying the seed to be sown,
they shall come back rejoicing, carrying their sheaves.

PSALM 126

— 11 —

Resurrection

They came to Jericho. And as he was leaving Jericho with his disciples and a sizable crowd, Bartimaeus, a blind man, the son of Timaeus, sat by the roadside begging. On hearing that it was Jesus of Nazareth, he began to cry out and say, "Jesus, son of David, have pity on me." And many rebuked him, telling him to be silent. But he kept calling out all the more, "Son of David, have pity on me." Jesus stopped and said, "Call him." So they called the blind man, saying to him, "Take courage; get up, he is calling you." He threw aside his cloak, sprang up, and came to Jesus. Jesus said to him in reply, "What do you want me to do for you?" The blind man replied to him, "Master, I want to see." Jesus told him, "Go your way; your faith has saved you." Immediately he received his sight and followed him on the way.

(Mk 10:46–52)

The final healing of your grief is coming soon. The wound has closed over. The pain is only occasional now, and it is no longer sharp. There is a scar, but it too will fade in time.

You stand at the edge of the "normal" world and know that you can now return to it. There is only one task left between you and resurrection. You must put down your grief and be willing to leave it behind.

Like Bartimaeus you have called out for help. Like Bartimaeus you have felt the nearness of the Lord and have heard his gentle question, "What do you want me to do for you?" But there is a little hook in the story, one that is easy to overlook, but one that is necessary for your healing. Mark says, "He threw aside his cloak, jumped up, and came to Jesus."

What we often don't realize is that to a blind beggar in the Palestine of two thousand years ago, a cloak was everything he had in life: blanket, pillow, shelter from the rain, shade from the sun, overcoat in the cold. It was *all* he had.

As you move through the landscape of grief, your sorrow begins to feel as if it were all you had, the only reality in a too changed world. It proves you once had someone close. It proves you loved. And you begin to cling to it.

But Jesus is calling now, gently insisting that you come to him unburdened so that he may envelop you in his final healing touch. Cast down your cloak and go to him. Leave it behind, all that suffering and sorrow, and go to him. Hear him say so softly that only you can hear him, "What do you want me to do for you?"

"Jesus," you reply, "I want to see again. I want to see color and beauty. I want to hear music. I want to taste the good things of earth. I want to love. I want to live."

And you will hear Jesus say, "Be on your way! Your faith has healed you."

A New Creation

You will step, healed and free, back into the land of the living. You will realize that you have undergone a change, but also that there is still meaning and purpose to your life. You are a new creation and that means new possibilities for you. You will find that the crisis through which you passed was not only the end of a time but also the beginning of one.

The continuing paradox of Christianity is that "unless a grain of wheat falls to the earth and dies, it remains just a grain of wheat. But if it dies, it produces much fruit" (Jn 12:24). As the one you loved is now producing great fruit in eternity, so you are now able to do so here on earth.

Though you pick up some of the old pieces of your life, your healed self will find new shapes and patterns in which to assemble them. It doesn't mean forgetting. But it does mean anticipating. And that means wellness. And life!

You will form new relationships and perhaps redefine old ones. You will discover that your capacity for love and joy are not diminished. You will take that final step out of the land of mourning to resurrection.

My prayer for you is that you will continue in the Lord's peace and joy and bring his message of comfort to others when they are in need. Being Ruth, the faithful one (see next chapter) is one of the most important ministries we can carry out for others.

May God continue to bless you and keep you close to himself.

PRAYER

O great God
—Creator, Redeemer, Sanctifier—
I thank you for the gift of my life.
I thank you for having been with me
in my pain, my loss, my loneliness.
I thank you for taking away my guilt and my fears.
I thank you for healing me,
for freeing me for life again.

Be with me still,
a constant source of love and peace.
Be at my side whatever comes.
Be near me.

Holy God, I praise your name with all my heart.

I lift up my eyes toward the mountains,
whence shall help come to me?
My help is from the Lord, who made heaven and earth.

May he not suffer my foot to slip,
may he slumber not who guards me.
Indeed he neither slumbers nor sleeps,
the guardian of Israel.

The Lord is my guardian; the Lord is my shade;
he is beside me at my right hand.
The sun shall not harm me by day,
nor the moon by night.

The Lord will guard me from all evil;
he will guard my life.
The Lord will guard my coming and my going,
both now and forever.

PSALM 121

— 12 —

Being Ruth

♦

> Naomi then ceased to urge (Ruth), for she saw she was determined to go with her.... Thus it was that Naomi returned with the Moabite daughter-in-law, Ruth, who accompanied her back from the plateau of Moab. They arrived in Bethlehem at the beginning of the barley harvest.
>
> (Ruth 1:18, 22)

Just as Ruth refused to leave Naomi's side but accompanied her on her journey and back to her homeland, so we may be called to be Ruth for someone else who is in mourning. Our initial feeling is probably one of helplessness. What do I say? What do I do?

What follows is a sort of compilation of do's and don'ts which have come together from the efforts of others and from the painfully garnered wisdom of my own experience. What it all comes down to is: be yourself, the loving friend you have always been. And don't let the bereaved's grief make you artificial, stilted, or — God forbid — absent.

For much of the material in this section I am indebted to Lee Schmidt of Parent Bereavement Outreach in Santa Monica, California, for "Helping the Bereaved Parent" and to the scores of those who have researched before me or shared their wisdom with me.

The Do's

Do let your genuine concern and caring show. There is nothing that reaches into the land of mourning quite so effectively as love.

Do be available — to listen, to run errands, to babysit, to do whatever is needed, and to listen some more.

Do say you are sorry about the death and about their pain. It's probably the most natural emotion you can have at this point.

Do allow them to express their grief, but only as they wish to and in the manner they desire. It is *their* grief and only they can make the decision of how much to express to you.

Do encourage them to be patient with themselves, not to expect themselves to do everything that they were able to do before under normal circumstances.

Do even encourage them to be especially good to themselves, to treat themselves to things that usually give them pleasure. But the word to remember is "encourage," not "force."

Do allow them to talk about the loved one who has died; as much and as often as they want to.

Do give special attention to mourning children, especially the "quiet ones," who are often overlooked in the pain and confusion of the moment. They feel everything the bereaved adult does but frequently need help in expressing it.

Do take notice of the father, if the death of a child has

taken place. He is often the forgotten parent in such cases while attention is focused on the grieving mother. His pain is as real, and he may have more trouble expressing it.

Do reassure the mourners that they did everything they could, that the medical care their loved one received was the best, or whatever else you know to be positive about the care given to the deceased.

Do use the words "death" and "dead." That is the reality. To say "passed on" or "gone to sleep" or "taken by God" sidesteps the truth. And, in the case of child mourners, it can give them frightening images of sleep or negative feelings about God which they might carry throughout their lives.

Do remember the "disenfranchised" mourner if your relationships allow for it. The stepmother or father, the ex-husband or wife is probably also experiencing grief at some level and can use comforting.

Do allow the griever to cry, to be angry, to shout, to do whatever is necessary to move the emotions out and away.

And *do* let your faith in God be a beacon for those in mourning. This is a time when the words of Jesus call out to us strongly.

> "You are the light of the world. A city set on a mountain cannot be hidden. Nor do they light a lamp and then put it under a bushel basket; it is set on a lamp stand where it gives light to all in the house. Just so, your light must shine before others so that they may see your good deeds and glorify your heavenly Father." (Mt 5:14–16)

They may not want to hear it, at least right away. But you can say it with your love and compassion. Even more than being Ruth, you can be Jesus for them in their grief.

The Don'ts

Don't let your own sense of helplessness keep you from reaching out. Those in grief feel a thousand times more helpless than you do. Trust that God will show you what you need to know, do, be during this time. My experience has taught me that he will.

Don't avoid them because you are uncomfortable. A little discomfort is a small price to pay for the gift of friendship.

Don't say you know how they feel unless you have experienced the same loss in your life. Until we have stood at the grave of a parent, a spouse, a lover, a child, we cannot know the feeling of those who have. And they know it.

Don't say, "You ought to be feeling better by now." We cannot make that judgment for anyone else because each person's grief is uniquely his or her own.

Don't tell them what they *should* be thinking or doing. There are no "shoulds" in grief.

Don't change the subject when they mention their dead loved one. Let them talk it out. Mourning has more than once been called "the talking cure." Don't try to suppress it.

Don't avoid mentioning the deceased's name out of fear of reminding them of their sorrow. They haven't forgotten it.

Don't promise to be there if you can't be. Your broken promise will be noticed. If you have made a commitment which you cannot keep, let the bereaved know and give an explanation. Don't believe that in their sorrow they will have forgotten. They may be depending on you.

And *don't* ever say, "Don't cry."

Remember Yourself as Well

Through all this companioning, remember to be patient with the griever and good to yourself. Walking with someone through mourning is sometimes exhausting and usually stressful. It is not easy to watch someone you care about hurt so deeply. Remember that, and take some time out for you.

And take some time for prayer. As we empty ourselves out in love and caring for another, only God can fill us up again. So take the time to be filled. And thank God that he is allowing you to be his instrument for others.

PRAYER

Gracious God,
I thank you for the blessing of my friends.
They need you now
and they need me to be you for them.

Please, fill me with your love, your grace,
your strength, your compassion
so that I may take this healing journey with them
and be a source of consolation on the way.

Give me your words to speak,
your ears to listen,
your heart to love.
Ease their pain, gentle Lord,
and heal their wounds.

A Final Word

I will heal them and lead them.
I will give full comfort
to them and to those who mourn for them,
I, the Creator, who gave them life.
Peace, peace to the far and near,
says the Lord, and I will heal them.

(Is 57:18–19)

There is one last thing that I would like to emphasize. Grieving is not something that you must do alone. In fact, talking it out helps to lessen the burden considerably. That's one thing friends do very well!

We are here, I believe with all my heart, to be friendship and compassion and healing love for one another. Never more so than in a time of great sorrow.

But perhaps you are truly alone. Through some unkind set of circumstances there is no one to whom you can turn.

Or perhaps your grief is so overwhelming that you feel you can't handle it.

What then?

Take heart, for the Lord has provided for you. There are people in the healing ministry, people in grief counseling who are only too willing to help you find your way back to wellness in company with the Lord.

Ask your pastor or your diocesan office of pastoral services for a name. You need not suffer this alone.

And though I do not know your name, be assured that you and all those who mourn will always be at the heart of my prayer.

About the Author

Sister Ruthann Williams, O.P., is a member of the Dominican Sisters of Caldwell, New Jersey. She holds a Master's Degree from Drew University (Literature) and a second Master's (Spirituality) from Immaculate Conception Seminary of Seton Hall University.

Sister has given retreats and days of recollection in New Jersey, New York, Pennsylvania, Massachusetts, California, Maine, Florida, Texas, Illinois, and Virginia. She has led pilgrimages to Israel and to Medugorje in the former Yugoslavia. Sister has an active women's ministry and leads many days of prayer and healing for women. For the past four years she has directed a national conference for women, held annually in the Northeast, and has appeared on cable television through the auspices of O.P. Productions.

Sister Ruthann's articles and poems have been published in regional and national magazines, most recently in *The Priest, Brothers,* and *Sisters Today* magazines, and in *Ruah,* a volume of poetry. An article which she wrote on pastoral care for the sexually addicted has been translated into several languages for worldwide distribution.

Sister's first book *Healing Your Grief* was published in 1987; her second *Go In Peace: Healing For Women* in 1990;

and *Thank You For Hearing My Call,* which she co-authored, also in 1990. In 1992 a small volume of her poetry, *Mystery,* was released. She also has a number of video and audio tapes in distribution.

A graphic artist and designer, Sister has won over one hundred regional and national awards for her work. In June 1991 she was further honored for her "Outstanding Work in Healing and Evangelization" at the national conference *Healed By Love.* And in June 1992 she was recognized for her pioneer work in women's ministry at a ceremony at Sacred Heart Cathedral in the Archdiocese of Newark, New Jersey.

Sister Ruthann is a member of the Association of Christian Therapists, the Christian Counselors Association, the Order of St. Luke, and the National Catholic Association for Communicators.

Published by Resurrection Press

A Rachel Rosary *Larry Kupferman*	$3.95
Catholic Is Wonderful *Mitch Finley*	$4.95
Common Bushes *Kieran Kay*	$8.95
Christian Marriage *John & Therese Boucher*	$3.95
Discovering Your Light *Margaret O'Brien*	$6.95
The Gift of the Dove *Joan M. Jones, PCPA*	$3.95
Healing through the Mass *Robert DeGrandis, SSJ*	$7.95
Healing Your Grief *Ruthann Williams, OP*	$7.95
His Healing Touch *Michael Buckley*	$7.95
Let's Talk *James P. Lisante*	$7.95
A Celebration of Life *Anthony Padovano*	$7.95
Miracle in the Marketplace *Henry Libersat*	$5.95
Heart Business *Dolores Torrell*	$6.95
A Path to Hope *John Dillon*	$5.95
Inwords *Mary Kraemer, OSF*	$4.50
The Healing of the Religious Life *Faricy/Blackborow*	$6.95
Transformed by Love *Margaret Magdalen, CSMV*	$5.95
RVC Liturgical Series: The Liturgy of the Hours	$3.95
The Lector's Ministry	$3.95
Behold the Man *Judy Marley, SFO*	$3.50
I Shall Be Raised Up	$2.25
In the Power of the Spirit *Kevin Ranaghan*	$6.95
Young People and... You Know What *William O'Malley*	$3.50
Lights in the Darkness *Ave Clark, O.P.*	$8.95
Practicing the Prayer of Presence *van Kaam/Muto*	$7.95
5-Minute Miracles *Linda Schubert*	$3.95
Nothing but Love *Robert Lauder*	$3.95
Faith Means... If You Pray for Rain, Bring an Umbrella *Antoinette Bosco*	$3.50
Stress and the Search for Happiness *van Kaam/Muto*	$3.95
Harnessing Stress *van Kaam/Muto*	$3.95
Healthy and Holy under Stress *van Kaam/Muto*	$3.95
Season of Promises *Mitch Finley*	$4.50
Stay with Us *John Mullin, SJ*	$3.95
Still Riding the Wind *George Montague*	$7.95
The Joy of Being a Catechist *Gloria Durka*	$3.95

Spirit-Life Audiocassette Collection

Hail Virgin Mother	*Robert Lauder*	$6.95
Praying on Your Feet	*Robert Lauder*	$6.95
Annulment: Healing-Hope-New Life	*Thomas Molloy*	$6.95
Life After Divorce	*Tom Hartman*	$6.95
Path to Hope	*John Dillon*	$6.95
Thank You Lord!	*McGuire/DeAngelis*	$8.95
Spirit Songs	*Jerry DeAngelis*	$9.95
Through It All	*Jerry DeAngelis*	$9.95

Resurrection Press books and cassettes are available in your local religious bookstore. If you want to be on our mailing list for our up-to-date announcements, please write or phone:

Resurrection Press
P.O. Box 248, Williston Park, NY 11596
1-800-89 BOOKS